CW00671646

'CHARL

THE CHARLIE WILLIAMS STORY

by

STEPHEN D SMITH

With Foreword by Ken Dodd

First published in Great Britain in 1998
by Neville-Douglas Publishing Ltd
Clumber Lodge, Hemingfield Road
Wombwell, Barnsley S73 OLY

To my friend Neil Crossland
and the memory of Keith H Clayton deceased.

Acknowledgements

Alamo Products, ©Danny Baker/The Times 20.06.98, BBC Radio Derby, BBC Radio Humberside, BBC Radio Leeds, BBC Radio Sheffield, Gordon & Iris Beecher, Tony Bluff, Duggie Brown, Sydney Bycroft, Philip Caplan, Tony Capstick, Duggie Chapman, Norman Collier, Robin Colvill, Roger de Courcey, Jimmy Cricket, Neil Crossland, Terry Dobson, Ken Dodd, Craig Douglas, Mike French, Sir David Frost, John Fulton, Christopher Good, The Grumbleweeds, John Hamp, Bill Harman, Haworth Graphics, Vince Hill, John Holmes, Alick Jeffrey, Michael Joseph, Stanley Joseph, Keresforth Hall Country Club, Bobby Knutt, Sir John Layden (deceased), Joe Longthorne, Beaulah and Michael Mann, Jeni Morton, Alan Oliver, Ross Parry Picture Agency, Billy Pearce, Len Pigott, Melvyn Prior, David and Linda Selley of Dapet Textiles, Ethel Smith, Rebecca Eve Smith, Jennifer M Smith, Ray Singleton, Stagewear Unlimited, Eric Todd, Max Tuoy, Wilford Smith Solicitors, Janice Williams, Rick Wakeman, Roy Walker, Judith Watts, Gary Wilmot, Sydney Wort and Yorkshire Television.

Stephen D Smith 1998
A CIP record for his book is available
from the British Library

ISBN 1 901853 50 0   Paperback

The right of Stephen D Smith to be identified as the Author of this work has been asserted by him in accordance with the copyright, Designs and Patents Act 1988 All rights reserved.   No part of this publication may be reproduced in any form or by any means, without permission from the publishers.

Printed in Great Britain by
Neville-Douglas Publishing Ltd
Clumber Lodge, Hemingfield Road, Wombwell,
Barnsley, Yorkshire S73 OLY

Contents

FOREWORD

Charlie Williams is the original item.   A natural comedian with a unique style.

He is right when he describes comedy as 'a serious business'.   It is an exploration of ideas and concepts and he is a master of his art.

This book is by a man who prefers not to dish the dirt or to seek controversy by causing embarrassment to participants in its pages, but it remains an affectionate and yet frank and open look at the life of one of the country's most popular comedians.

KEN DODD

PREFACE

When Neil Crossland asked me to write Charlie's biography I could not believe my luck! Charlie is famous nationally but where I come from in South Yorkshire he is a legend.

Ken Dodd has described this book as an affectionate look at the life of Charlie Williams, and he is right. If the reader is looking for skeletons to be dragged screaming from the closet and the innermost personal foibles laid bare for the voyeur, look elsewhere. This book describes the life of a truly great comedian of the old school who loved to make people laugh without resorting to bad taste to achieve his desire.

If I can be forgiven for indulging in the time-honoured tradition of offering thanks, I am grateful to everyone who has played a part in the preparation of this book but I would particularly like to mention Neil Crossland who not only made it possible for me to write this book, but has helped me in so many ways with his time and effort. I would also like to thank Janice, Charlie's wife, for her kindness and hospitality throughout so many visits to her beautiful home and last but by no means least, Charlie himself for living up to his reputation as a very nice man and allowing me to become his friend and understand why no-one had a bad word to say about him.

Stephen D Smith

Chapter 1

"You Want to Write a Biography?"
"If swearing was funny we'd all be comics."
Charlie Williams

It was Thursday 30th October 1997 at 8.30pm, a strong burst of light illuminated the well manicured lawn and the path where I was standing. A familiar face wearing a large beaming smile greeted me from beneath the security light.

"Alreight me old flower," said my host as I was beckoned into the warm glow of the front porch. I felt welcome.

I was accompanied by Neil Crossland, an old friend of mine who was managing Charlie's retirement as well as his own stagewear business, making a considerable success of both. Neil had been Charlie's close friend for almost as many years as he had been mine, but I had lost touch with him for ten years until only the week before this meeting, when circumstances dictated a renewal of our friendship.

It was one of those quirks of fate which was to lead me to write the biography of one of Britain's finest comedians. Neil had read my book 'Boozers Ballcocks & Bail' whilst on holiday in Greece and thankfully he had liked it. He believed that the time was right to record Charlie's story for posterity and if he, Charlie, liked the idea, I was in. This was to be a most important meeting. Charlie showed us into his tastefully furnished conservatory and drinks arrived by courtesy of his wife

Janice. We talked for three hours. We were all agreed it was a story of a life of experiences rich in humour and achievement and all the better for telling.

I had expected somewhat erroneously that I would be treated to a flurry of jokes, but Charlie was contemplative and keen to listen to what I had to say. He was just short of his seventieth birthday, and but for his white hair, he had worn well, but on leaving I saw that some measure of infirmity had taken hold of that once athletic frame proving that arthritis does not discriminate between individuals. Charlie had not avoided the curse of one of the most cruel of conditions which had played such a crucial role in his decision to retire from full-time entertaining.

I had seen Charlie at his best in the sixties, seventies and eighties when a television career beckoned the former miner and professional footballer and so I was looking forward to hearing him again to assess if time had played tricks upon my memory. He had a unique place in the comedy Hall of Fame, quite a paradox for a coloured man with a heavily pronounced Yorkshire accent and a penchant for making people laugh. What intrigued me most was the mechanics of his personality. What really made him tick? What did he think of today's comedians? What did he think of yesterday's comedians? Who were his heroes, both in sport and entertainment? And what of race? How hard had it been for a black man to break into that which had predominantly been a white male preserve?

It would require a special kind of man with such so-called 'disadvantages' to succeed against the prejudices of those times and here he was and here was my opportunity to play my part in the attempt to answer all those questions.

I was to start work by attending one of Charlie's shows which Neil had arranged at the hotel in Doncaster. It was a charity function with Charlie as top of the bill. I was to be an interested observer, taking notes and recording conversations whilst sitting unobtrusively backstage whilst the master weaved his magic to an audience of devotees. I was not to be disappointed.

Arrangements had been made to arrive at the hotel by approximately 8.15pm, when we would be taken to a makeshift dressing-room, converted from one of the rooms close to the banqueting hall where the guests were assembled.

The event was a charity dinner in aid of a young girl who required a very expensive operation in America because our own National Health scheme had failed her. The organiser, Alan Oliver, had arranged the show and had called upon Neil to secure Charlie's services.

Alan greeted us at the hotel and carefully placed traffic cones were removed to secure parking directly outside the front door. It was interesting to see the look of reverence on so many faces as Charlie got out of the car. It was a look I was to witness in others time and time again as I travelled with Charlie to various venues in search of material for the book.

We entered the hotel and whilst walking through the foyer I saw many a head turn and look in recognition as we walked towards the lift. I am not sure if Charlie noticed the reaction, but if he did, he didn't say so. The lift came to a halt with a bump.

"Bloody 'ell," announced Charlie. "I'll be two inches

shorter now."

The door opened and we made our way to the dressing-room which was indeed makeshift. There was no drawing of a star on the door and the inside was full of clothing belonging to the two other artistes who were performing that night. It was interesting that Charlie made no complaint; there was no sign of temperament, a feature of so many artistes. But then Charlie had nothing to prove.

The manager was brought in to meet us and as he entered, his attentions were focused upon his star guest.

"Good evening Mr Williams, I'm very pleased to meet you," said the manager shaking his hand.

"All reight me old flower," replied Charlie using the catch-phrase greeting which we had all come to expect.

"Can I offer you a drink?" he asked pleasantly.

"I thought you'd never ask!" said Charlie smiling and only moments later the manager arrived with our drinks including a whisky and lemonade delivered into an appreciative but arthritic hand.

It was 8.30pm and the manager left us to supervise the dinner. Charlie reached for his bag and brought out a small but neat parcel wrapped in red cloth. It was a hip flask. I watched as Charlie unscrewed the container and added the contents to his glass.

"I don't like ice," said Charlie, "It waters it down too much so I'll liven it." He poured a small measure into the glass before handing it to me. Charlie asked me to wrap it up in the red piece of velvet cloth and return it to his bag, pointing to the position specially reserved for the purpose.

"What time is it?" asked Charlie.

"8.35pm," I replied.

"I'm on at 10," said Charlie, "so it's time for our meal."

His reference to the time and the request for the ritualistic wrapping of the flask indicated to me that Charlie was an exact type of character. He liked his clothes on a hanger with his bow-tie, dress suit and patent shoes at the ready. He believed that bad time keeping was professionally unacceptable. He preferred to be early for everything to enable him to gather his thoughts and so hated being late. Another guest then arrived seeking an audience. It was the assistant manager, a young woman in her twenties who had called to check upon our welfare. She studied Charlie carefully as she suggested the menu.

"It's a turkey dinner," she said brightly.

"I'll have a sandwich," said Charlie, deflating her somewhat. "It's the turkey season, we'll be given it for every meal, so I'll have a sandwich please. I can't do with too much turkey."

"Certainly," said the assistant manager, "and you gentlemen?"

Neil and I both agreed upon the hot meal which someone else ate for me whilst I was escorted to the stage area to conduct the auction of showbusiness memorabilia collected specially for the event.

I had never conducted an auction before and so I asked Neil why I had been chosen to perform the duty. He told me that he had never dealt with an auction before either and that was it. I still haven't had a satisfactory explanation, but nevertheless I soldiered on, in an attempt to sell all sorts of items which had been donated by various celebrities. There were autographed footballs and pennants, and even one of Rick Wakeman's concert jackets, but the one item which I had difficulty selling was an autographed framed photograph of that great character actor from *Last of the Summer Wine*, Jane Freeman.

After every three or four items were sold I would reintroduce the photograph to the auction, but without success. I even told them that it was a 'collector's item' and could be worth a great deal of money at some stage in the future. One wag from the audience shouted, "Well, you buy it then!"

The auction finished at 10.20pm and I returned to the dressing-room with my hair dampened with sweat and my voice hoarse after half an hour of cajoling a gently intoxicated audience out of some of their well-earned cash.

When I returned to the dressing-room Charlie was ready; resplendent in his dress suit and patent shoes. He nodded and smiled as I entered but he was unhappy about the delay and he prompted Neil about the time. I really wanted to know if Charlie suffered from nerves but I thought the question presumptuous, doubting whether he would have appreciated such a query at that time, despite the role I was fulfilling. If I was to witness a chink in the armour it was then when the manager appeared and told Charlie it was time.

"Right-oh," said Charlie, "Let's get to it. Hey Neil, is me tie straight?", he asked nervously.

"Certainly is," said Neil thoughtfully. "Oh, you are handsome," he said with a smile.

"I didn't know you cared," replied Charlie and then the group walked along the corridor and into the kitchen which led to the banqueting hall. Charlie greeted the assembled staff in his inimitable fashion.

"All reight my flowers?" he shouted.

It was interesting to see their reaction which was most positive if a little hesitant, but I recognised the same look of reverence which I had seen earlier upon our arrival.

I took my place at a table and waited for Charlie's act to begin. Neil was standing nervously in the entrance to the stage with Charlie by his side waiting for the compere Lee Sinclair to make his introduction. A stool was placed on the stage and the lights were dimmed as Lee began to speak.

"And now ladies and gentlemen, it is an honour for me to introduce you to a comedy legend. Please welcome on stage the one and only Charlie Williams............"

Charlie was greeted by a huge round of applause as he stepped back, half sitting and half standing by the stool.

"All reight my flowers? Good evening, ladies and gentlemen. Welcome to my country."

Charlie addressed the audience as though they were his friends, regaling them with stories from slapstick to race. There were no swear words or bouts of smut but only the slightest innuendo, rather like that of the popular seaside postcard.

He told the audience of one of his first relationships with the opposite sex, explaining and apologising for his youthful naivety.

"The first time we had a liaison was embarrassing for us both. After it was over I confessed that had I known she was a virgin I would not have taken advantage. She told me that had she known I was going to take advantage she would have taken her tights off!"

Charlie was in control and the audience were in the palm of his hand.

The gremlins in the sound system started to taunt him as he entered the final phase of his act, first a whistle and then an ever-increasing rumble.

"Bloody 'ell, it'll frighten me to death," said Charlie as he tilted the offending microphone forwards repeatedly as if making a blessing. The audience continued to laugh at Charlie's mock annoyance at the sound engineer who crept onto the stage in search of the offending electrical defect.

"I'm going to get that lad a job," announced Charlie, and after a suitable pause........

"Aye, down Maltby colliery.........in place of the canaries!"

More laughter and with it Charlie had addressed a simple but potentially embarrassing fault with a microphone. He had learned his trade well. He was the epitome of the stand-up comic with a flawless technique and above all originality which had made this ex-miner from Royston, Barnsley, a household name.

Originality had manifested itself in the form of a black man telling jokes about colour prejudice in a strong South Yorkshire accent, a contradiction in terms possibly, but eye-catching and thought provoking certainly. He was a talking point and with his talent and a genuinely nice nature, he told stories of real life which helped audiences to empathise with him. I was beginning to see for myself how Charlie had become a great success, but more importantly how he had managed to sustain it during a glittering thirty year career.

The conclusion of his act met with great applause. It

was an expression not only of pleasure but of appreciation, affection and respect for this most charming of men. I too had been captivated and found myself standing with the other members of the audience in tribute.

He left the stage to shouts of admiration and the compere called him back to take a bow. I remembered one of his favourite phrases just at that moment, "You have to *earn* respect lad," and of course he was right. I saw it as my task to embark upon a most pleasant and enjoyable journey, recalling a life of hardship and sacrifice of a man who taught us to laugh at the evils of bigotry and prejudice.

I went backstage to offer my congratulations to find a queue of admirers all congregated in the small room. They all had something to say, remembering where and when they had seen Charlie before. He was expected to recall the most obscure of meetings but he was courteous to them all, and I got the distinct impression that he was actually enjoying and appreciating the attention.

"Aren't people nice," he announced as the last visitor left allowing him to change. I decided it would be prudent to leave to allow him to undress, but Charlie bade me stay as he explained,

"It's not true what they say about black men tha' knows," he said with a cheeky smile, unfastening the top of his trousers. "I were at back of the queue when they were dished out," he continued. I laughed and excused myself to go in search of my meal and a drink. I missed out on the former but more than made up for it with the latter. Minutes later Charlie came out into the audience and sat as admirers wandered up to his table in search of an audience and an autograph. Charlie spoke to each one in turn, leaving only when the volume of the guest singer made it too difficult to hold a conversation.

"He's a lovely man," said one young woman who was standing in the queue at the bar. I estimated she was in her twenties, born at the time when Charlie's popularity was at its height. She was a thoroughly modern miss, beautifully dressed in the latest fashions with a good looking face, beautifully groomed hair and well manicured nails.

"It's so nice to listen to a comedian who doesn't swear and tell jokes about women's periods and gynaecological problems," she continued. For a moment I felt all of my forty-nine years as I agreed with her, particularly when she pointed out that the old timers were the best.

"I bet you grew up with him," said one interested by-stander listening to our conversation.

I simply smiled and nodded in agreement in the realisation that the silly bugger must have thought that Charlie and I were of a similar age. I whispered something under my breath as he walked away but it was difficult to smile and swear at the same time.

"Some bugger had me and you at the same age," I said to Charlie on my return to the dressing-room. "It makes you look good," I said with a hearty laugh.

"Aye, but it doesn't say much for thee," said Charlie turning the joke against me.

We enjoyed a last drink before making our farewells. I left with some fond memories of the evening, which was to be the basis of the first chapter of the book, and a signed photograph of Jane Freeman which had been presented to me by the organiser. I picked up Charlie's suit and made for the car. I was last out and as I reached for the light switch, I noticed an uneaten turkey sandwich resting on the table. It seemed that neither of us ate that evening.

I started work in earnest, just before Christmas of 1997, with the first of one of our many meetings. The game plan was to meet regularly and discuss the past. I would arrive at Charlie's house, on time of course, and we would talk until lunch-time, interrupted only by Janice who kindly kept us supplied with tea, sandwiches and biscuits.

The first meeting was on December 10th and Charlie related a number of stories about his very many showbusiness friends. I even had access to the 'big red book' presented after Charlie appeared on the *This is Your Life* television programme. There were photographs and memorabilia of all shapes and sizes and letters and telegrams of congratulations marking Charlie's retirement, from such big notables as Shirley Bassey, Roger D'Courcey, Tommy Steele and so very many more.

All the material was there, if not in Charlie's head then adorning his study wall.

As the old cliché says, what better place to start than at the beginning, but perhaps to gain a greater understanding of Charlie's heritage, we have to look back a little further into the life of his forebears and particularly his father who played such an important and crucial role in Charlie's formative years. So our story starts with the life and times of Charlie's dad, Charles Augustus Williams, born in Barbados in the West Indies, circa 1879.

Chapter Two

ESCAPE FROM BARBADOS

Barbados was settled by Englishmen in 1627 and had never been under any other flag until it became independent in 1966. It is the easternmost West Indian island which lies about 250 miles north-east of Venezuela. It is one of the most densely populated countries in the world. The island was inhabited by Caribs who were short yellow-skinned straight-haired people with markedly Mongolian features and are believed to have been descended from Mongols, who migrated from Asia across the Bering Straight tens of thousands of years ago. The Aboriginal Carib race has almost disappeared from the West Indian Islands, but a remnant still survives in the Island of the Dominican Republic.

The early European settlers intended to farm the lands themselves as they had done in their home countries and for a generation they did so successfully, but mistaken ideas on the dignity of race, coupled with a certain laziness that the perpetual warmth of the climate induced, prompted them to avoid manual work and they imported slaves from Africa to do it for them. In time, tne latter's descendants far out-numbered the Europeans. At the turn of the century the population of the West Indies was predominantly of African race with a considerable mixture of European blood.

Slavery had come to an end in the British West Indies with the passing of legislation on 1st August 1834, but the aftermath of slavery was still present.   Professor T S Simey, who was the advisor on Social Services to the Comptroller for Development and Welfare in the West Indies in the 1940's, referred to the state of affairs in his book Welfare and Planning in the West Indies.   He explained,

"The prevailing type of West Indian which is encountered over and over again in all the colonies, is very loose in organisation.   It is rarely founded on the ceremony of marriage and the relationships between its members are often very casual indeed.   There is little control over the children, who may receive plenty of maternal affection (tempered by explosions of emotion), but little in the way of careful general upbringing."

He went on to say that slavery was the most potent force in causing this result,

"The begetting of children was a function to be encouraged in every way.   The maternal instincts of the mother were an economic asset, but the bearing of responsibilities as a husband or a father could only be regarded as a distraction from field labour.   Family life of the western type was an impossibility.   The buying and selling of slaves involved the splitting-up of families."

At the turn of the century, the illegitimacy rates common throughout the West Indies, varied from sixty to seventy-five per cent of the total number of births.   Professor Simey who had studied the Island, pointed out that the relationship between parents was generally a fleeting one, explaining that the man was more often the wanderer.

Progress on the island was slow and much needed to be done.   The prospects of education were limited, especially amongst the lower classes. Slavery had been as corrupting of the lives of the masters as it was of the slaves. In the first place British people settled in the colonies with the intention of farming the land themselves, but by abandoning that purpose and substituting slave labour for their own, they accepted defeat and dependence on another race to provide them with a living. Insecurity bred fears and fear bred cruelty. Charles' life was not to be free of it until he was to leave the Island.

The colonies had been tied more and more to one product, namely sugar, and when its price collapsed in the latter half of the nineteenth century, the West Indies were unable to substitute other crops more profitable than sugar, because sugar alone would provide sufficient employment for the population.

The effects of slavery on the morals of the masters and their descendants were moreover disastrous. Ownership of women who were thus completely in their power, gave rise to sexual laxity which extended into relatively recent times of which the proof lies in the shades of brown between black and white, more commonly seen in those colonies than either black or white.

In 1898 The United States of America, which was the principal market for the British West Indian sugar, granted Cuban sugar a preference in the American market. A period of acute depression followed and with it considerable strife. The most striking fact about the West Indian people was their poverty and even as late as the 1940's the annual earnings of agricultural workers in Barbados was nothing more than twenty to twenty-five pounds per year.

Charlie's father, Charles Augustus Williams, was born in Barbados on St Patrick's Day, the 17th March 1879. He was a member of a large family who adopted the name of the plantation owner where they worked. The realities of being one of a large and poor family without a surname of their own doubtless played its part in Charles' search for an identity, which led him to run away to sea at the age of fourteen. Little is known of his formative years in Barbados as there are no records and he spoke very little of it, save only to wax lyrical of the Island's beauty.

Charles worked on the sugar cane plantation with his father and brothers just as soon as he could walk and carry the cane, but his prospects were limited to working in the fields and a hovel in which to live. There was little wonder that Charles' mind wandered as he looked out to sea and observed the tall ships making their way to and from the harbour laden with cane for far-off lands.

There was little to occupy his thoughts as he worked in the heat of the sun, but Charles dreamed dreams and he wondered what it would be like on the far side of the horizon, where the sun rested gently before disappearing to bring light and warmth to other continents.

Week after week, month after month, year after year, Charles worked in the fields. The cycle was simple, work and then sleep and then work again, interspersed only by meals and the company of a family inundated with relatives bearing the same surname. He was related to most of the people with whom he had contact and he had numerous cousins who were either once or twice removed. Despite the beauty of the Island with continual warmth, disturbed only by the gentle sea breeze, Charles was frustrated by his desire for travel and a yearning to live a different life from that with which he had become accustomed. With an ever-growing awareness of the world beyond from stories told by the sailors at the waterfront, Charles wrestled with his loyalties to his family and his desire to satisfy his longing to see the world. Inevitably the time came when Charles decided that his future lay away from his island home and the siren call to adventure proved too strong to resist.

His intention was to seek his fortune, but it was a world neither ready nor able to favour acceptance of a black man into anything other than menial work. Charles had no particular skills and his illiteracy was to limit his prospects, but with an indomitable spirit and more than average intelligence he fled the West Indian shores, never to return. He seized his opportunity at the Bridgetown dock, enrolling with a merchant steamer as a cabin boy after lying about his age to get the job. Charles was to spend the next twenty years travelling the world, gaining a considerable insight into the workings of its peoples.

It appears that he was happy in the merchant navy and with his sense of humour and infectious laugh he made many friends. He would speak of his journeys with great pride to eager and avid listeners far removed from witnessing firsthand the glories of travel.

In 1914 Charles' wanderings brought him to England and the start of World War One. He was a handsome man, over six feet tall and weighing between seventeen and eighteen stones. He was extremely strong, fearless and a most suitable candidate for the forces. The enlistment posters beckoned and what proved to be the nemesis for so many, provided an opportunity of experience for Charles which was impossible to resist. Entranced by the promises of glory, Charles enlisted in the Royal Engineers and within a matter of days found himself in the realities and horror of the trenches in the Somme. He was no stranger to hardship and difficult living conditions and so he found it relatively easy to comply with the rigours and discipline of life in the forces, but the memories of the futility of war and the obscenity of death in conflict were to live with him for ever.

He served the Allies well and was decorated for bravery in the face of enemy fire, but his modesty forbade him to talk of it and the 'secret' was only uncovered from a chance meeting with one of his former compatriots. He was a very brave man who achieved great popularity amongst his fellow soldiers with whom he had shared such adversity.

He was lucky. He managed to survive the war without suffering the ignominy of wounds, but like so many others he was left with a legacy of frostbite and a condition with the unpleasant sounding name of 'trench feet' which was to haunt him for the remainder of his life. It was said that Charles arrived on the southern shores of England after the end of the war having fought in that most terrible of wars without perhaps knowing the meaning or the reason for it. Perhaps it was an escape, but fate had decreed that he would see the savage encounters of mankind's inhumanity towards his fellow man and live through the experience to tell the tale. He arrived, as did the many, to a heroes welcome and little else except a nation's gratitude served by a short memory.

Formal education had eluded him as had the ability to read and write, but he was large and powerfully built with the strength of two men, and what he lost in learning he more than made up for with common sense. He travelled north working en route to pay for his keep, and although it is not generally believed that South Yorkshire was his target, he settled in Royston, a small mining village near Barnsley. Eventually with the money he had earned performing all manner of menial jobs, he bought a horse and cart for the purveying of groceries, utilising his endearing personality as a considerable aid to his sales technique.

In his daily tutorials about life, he would often tell Charlie that his colour had never been a problem, because in those days there were very few black men on these shores. He had always taken the view that prejudice and bigotry were born out of fear and while ever there were only a few of his kind, prejudice was unlikely to play a substantial part in his life, but he also believed that an ever increasing number of immigrants would create fear amongst the endogenous population and he was right.

Charles was a philosopher and had a keen sense of understanding of his fellow man but despite his size and power he was rarely in a situation where his physical talents had to be used. He would often say,

"A fight only means you have to buy a new suit."

He saw no point in buying suits unnecessarily, but if the chips were down and no alternative could be found he was more than a match for any would-be aggressor. He lived in an age where the blackman was a novelty but novelties always had an appeal, especially to the female population. This is where Charlie's mother came in.

Chapter Three

EARLY DAYS

C harles met Doris Cook, a South Yorkshire girl at a dance in the church hall in Royston near Barnsley and an association developed. She had a son called Alvin by a previous union but he had long since lived with relatives which left Doris free to further her liaison with Charles.

Charlie was the first born of the relationship, on 23rd December 1927, at a time when the country was trying to come to terms with the aftermath of the General Strike. It was provoked by a dispute in the coal industry and was designed to compel the government to intervene and enforce on the employers the acceptance of terms in the coal industry favourable to the workers. Unemployment ravaged the country and no more so than in the north of England when Charlie was born in Cross Lane, Royston, near Barnsley, South Yorkshire; but from what he has been told, he was a good, strong baby with no health problems. Doris, his sister, who was named after her mother, was born two years later but it appears that his mother suffered from postnatal depression, a condition much misunderstood in those days. Her condition deteriorated and she suffered a nervous breakdown with the result that she was taken into the local workhouse/hospital and then into a home to be cared for, which robbed young Charlie of the kind of care and support which only a mother can bring. The pressures of working full-time and being a single parent with no support or assistance meant that Charles was unable to care for two children, and so consequently his sister Doris went to live with an aunt, and thereafter into a children's home.   It was one of the tragedies quite common in those days of austerity where hardship begot suffering both physical and mental.   Charlie lost contact with Doris for many years and it was not until he was nineteen years old that their paths crossed again, their introduction being organised by Alvin, Charlie's half-brother, who knew of the existence of a half-brother and a half-sister and had decided to try to find them. Eventually he achieved his quest and for the first time they all met up together.   It was a joyous meeting.

Doris now lived in a hostel and Charlie returned her visits on a fairly regular basis travelling firstly alone and then with friends, to be eventually accompanied by a busload of acquaintances.   At first he thought they were just being supportive but the fact that Doris was living in an all female hostel may have had something to do with it. She eventually acquired a cottage in Doncaster and when Charlie began his footballing career he stayed with her at regular intervals.   Charlie had little contact with his mother who spent the majority of her time in and out of hospital and with relatives, but Charles was a good and caring father who gave his son the very best he could, not only of care and affection, but also the benefits of a gentle indoctrination into the sayings and beliefs which have played such an important part in forming Charlie's character.   There can be no doubt that a very special bond existed between father and son, enhanced perhaps by the absence of the mother figure in their home life.

Charlie was subsequently re-united with his mother but it was not until his marriage in 1957 that he was to see her again.

Home was at 12 Lakes Buildings, South Hiendley in a 'two-up, two-down' terraced house belonging to a private landlord where the 'bathroom' was to be found 'on a six inch nail hanging on the back door'. It was a portable tin bath, which came off the nail every Friday night.

There was a copper boiling pan in the corner of the kitchen with a ladling can to transport hot water into the bath but it was always a risky business getting the temperature right, for on occasions Charlie was unable to sit in it for fear of 'burning my goolies in the hot water'. If there was a shortage of hot water the bath had to be shared, which did not present a problem provided the other occupant had a sense of humour. Aromatherapy took the form of a half pound bar of carbolic soap which had a variety of duties, including washing-up, cleaning collars and clothes and of course the event of the week, bath night!

Charles was a good cook and Charlie was the only child in the neighbourhood who tasted the delights of curry for his tea, and his friends would often remark about the strange concoction whose aroma permeated the air and lingered for passers-by to savour. Charles had acquired considerable skill in the area of culinary endeavour when he had served with the Merchant Navy and tasted and learned of the great cuisines of the world, but the majority of Charlie's meals were prepared by a kindly neighbour, one Mrs Broadbent, who lived in one of the colliery homes nearby. Provisions were delivered by horse and cart, not because of the quantity they bought but because the tradesmen made their deliveries by a horse and cart!

Entertainment was provided by the childhood games of the day; the whip and top, 'Jack Shine a Light' and 'Kick out Can', but in winter, board games replaced outdoor pursuits with ludo and draughts being the most popular. Charlie became the focal point of attention one Christmas when he acquired a train set which made him the most popular kid on the block and most of the local kids craved his attention. It was a simple life with the philosophy of 'what you never had you never missed' and there was a uniformity amongst the villagers because they were all miners from similar families where few people stood out except perhaps shopkeepers, colliery deputies and 'bookies'. No-one had any more or any less than anyone else and so they all got on.

There were many hardships with the ever-present spectre of illness haunting society caused by a mixture of poor conditions and an insufficiency of nutrition in the diet.

The health service was not as it is now so that whooping cough and scarlet fever claimed lives with an alarming degree of regularity, but Charlie was lucky and managed to reach puberty relatively unscathed, although they were certainly difficult times and the miners needed to be tough to survive.

Whilst Charles was a loving and caring father, he was also a disciplinarian, teaching his son respect for his fellow man. "Respect earns respect," he used to say and of course Charlie had seen the benefits of that philosophy for his father was a well-liked and respected man. Evenings were spent with his father at home who told stories of his youth and far off lands that Charlie could barely imagine as he listened intently to stories of Barbados with its fine sandy beaches and its shelves of coral. His favourite memory was of tales of fishing for flying fish in the delightful coves around the island, whilst the heat of the sun played tricks upon the fishermen coping with the haze. Travellers often speak fondly of their homelands, Charles being no exception, and although considerable gloss may have been added in the telling, it gave inestimable pleasure to his captivated son who had inherited his father's ability to dream. Charles on the other hand sat with consummate pride as each night his son painstakingly read aloud the newspaper – something of an achievement as Charles saw it, for his son was the first of the Williams' clan with the ability to read and write.

Charles rarely showed aggression, although his earlier life in the trenches would have given him an excuse. It was not in his nature; but on one occasion the village bully with too much drink in his bloated stomach ran into him with villainy in mind and aggression in his heart. Insults were hurled at Charles together with the invitation to fight but the trauma was made greater to bear by young Charlie being present to witness the ordeal. Charles turned away and refused to fight, leaving Charlie open-mouthed in despair at what he thought was his father's cowardice. When the aggressor took an iron bar and made as if to make an attack, Charles reacted. He took the iron bar from his assailant and using his tremendous strength he bent the bar double before returning it to the bully in silent rebuke. The bully turned and walked away, leaving Charles' dignity intact and his suit undamaged by the experience. He took young Charlie's hand and wandered off about his business without so much as a word. The incident made a profound impact upon young Charlie, so much so that he was never to forget it.

Charles was a thoughtful and kindly man but unfortunately the legacy of the memories from those terrible years in the trenches was to haunt him, as it did so many others, and the malady of 'trench feet' would continue to taunt and provoke him whenever cold and damp conditions prevailed. It was a debilitating condition and at its height would necessitate Charlie's absence from school to concentrate on the day-to-day household tasks whilst his father was confined to his bed. Inevitably at night there were the nightmares when imaginary shells and cannons exploded in his head, tormenting his sleep and leaving him exhausted and even more susceptible to infirmity. Charlie's education suffered and his scholastic performance was blighted, but like his father he more than made up for it with common sense and an endearing ready wit.

Charlie's memory of his childhood begins when he was six years old, but despite the vagaries of youth he remembers his first school at South Hiendley where he met Gordon Beecher. Gordon Beecher is Charlie's lifelong school-friend with whom he has enjoyed and still enjoys a long-lasting and most rewarding friendship. They were both five years of age when they first met at the infants school and Gordon has fond memories of those days, recalling that Charlie was the only black child in a school of over three hundred and forty pupils. Although he has no recollection of any prejudice, he certainly remembers that there was bullying in the school, but it was not aimed at any specific individual. Gordon remembers being bullied by an older boy called Billy Beggs, and on one occasion he was with Charlie when Beggs reared his ugly head. He forced young Gordon to eat four birds' eggs under threat of being shot with an air pistol if he didn't and he remembers having to carry out the act whilst Charlie looked on gritting his teeth and biting his tongue.

"Charlie could stand no more and so he picked up a brick and threw it at the bully to distract his attention. Needless to say he turned on Charlie and chased him, which took him away from me, and put Charlie in peril, but Charlie had a good set of legs and he showed Beggsy some very clean heels, so he couldn't catch him."

It was a small example of friendship which Gordon has not forgotten and he recalls stories of boyhood larks where on Saturday afternoons the local population prepared the week's baking. They would make oven-bottom cakes and place them covered by a tea-towel on the window ledge, overlooking the 'backs' to cool. Gordon and Charlie became extremely adept at reaching up and removing the said cakes without consent, much to the annoyance of whoever baked them. Gordon remembers that Mr Williams senior was 'a very clever man who knew an awful lot about so many things'. He noted however that he was extremely strict and Charlie was keen not to get into his bad books.

Whilst they were very good times, Gordon remembers the poverty,

"There were no carpets in those days, just stone flags, and I always remember the cold and having to sit by a raging fire to keep warm. That's probably why the people were so tough, but then again I suppose they had to be."

Charlie's recollection of his teachers' names shows that the experience of school was marked indelibly on his memory. A pleasant lady called Miss Hoyland was his favourite; an understanding woman, she was Charlie's class teacher and from what he can remember she was sympathetic and kind and perhaps the mother substitute he had been seeking. They formed an alliance and she was quick to Charlie's defence if he was in trouble, but also found him bright and eager to learn. At eight years of age he was promoted to the middle school and then at eleven to the Ryhill Modern School.

At first, his colour was an advantage. He was a likeable rarity, and as an attractive child with a very friendly disposition, he courted considerable popularity. Colour was less of a problem for him than for anyone else, something which he was to turn to his advantage in later life both at work, in sport and on the stage but his profile had been relatively small until he began to show promise on the sports-field; then the trouble started. Sarcastic comments were first on the agenda followed by sniggering and then open abuse.

The school bully sought to find Charlie's Achilles heel and for the first time racial prejudice entered his life. Charlie remembered his father's words about fighting and he recalled the incident with the man who challenged his father with a weapon, but the circumstances were different.

"He didn't have an iron bar and I wouldn't have had the strength to have bent it if he had one, so I thought about my dad's teaching and when that failed, I cracked him."

"Fortunately," Gordon recalled, "Charlie was able to look after himself if he had to."
But he was very popular and it was never really a problem for him.
The bully was not to trouble him again but the taunts would return to haunt him from time to time from a variety of sources.
His academic career left much to be desired with his studies being interrupted by regular absences from school as his father's health deteriorated but he showed early promise in sport, particularly athletics.
There is always a fear of achievers, which can turn into an obsessive loathing by those who seemingly fall by the wayside and inevitably as Charlie's prowess increased so did the resentment from those who turned to colour prejudice to justify their stance but it was at school where he learned the power of lies, the price of experience and the agony of loss.
Charles was a witty man with a self-deprecating nature and young Charlie inherited his father's wit, which proved to be a useful ploy during those school years, alleviating more than one potentially nasty incident, but sport had given him strength and purpose and the ability to look after himself in the event of trouble. Gordon remembered Mr Williams senior as being a large powerful man whom the village respected. He was known affectionately in the locality as 'Black Charlie'. He was a strict disciplinarian and "When he said a thing, he meant it!" Charlie absorbed his father's humour at home and sport at school, fusing the two in the belief that

they were the keys to self-improvement.   His heroes of the day were the heavyweight boxing champion Joe Louis 'The Brown Bomber', Henry 'Homicide Hank' Armstrong, who was one of the first boxers to win world championships at different weights and the great American athlete Jesse Owens.   Significantly all three were black but they had hero status and were men who carried the cause of the black man with great dignity. Charlie's cousin Gerald Bedford was a keen amateur boxer and he introduced Charlie to the noble art, using him as a sparring partner in readiness for the N.C.B. amateur championships.

Charlie remembers the sparring sessions pointing out that the only problem was that "Gerald kept hitting me". Gerald's philosophy of 'retaliate first' proved useful in South Hiendley where self-preservation decreed that you had to be able to look after yourself.   Nevertheless the villagers were straight-talking and did not pull any punches and according to Charlie they were the 'salt of the earth'.

The best that can be said about Charlie's academic prowess was that he was good at sport.   Athletics and football were his favourite pastimes and he remembers a kindly man called Don Gordon who was the school games teacher - 'a fit bloke with a passion for football'. Charlie formed an affinity with his football coach and it wasn't long before he was in the football team, the cricket team and the captain of the school athletic squad. He was never happier than when he was standing his corner on the field of sporting endeavour and it was apparent to his teachers that Charlie might make the dizzy heights of a sporting career, but academia was something else.

Charlie would sit in his classroom with his unopened book before him whilst his classmates read out passages in turn, but his attention was focused on the playing field outside where boys ran and chased a football in search of make-shift goalposts created from jackets and jumpers of the class at play.   The classroom bell heralded a blessed release from the rigours of reading and writing and Charlie headed for the playground and the wide open spaces in which he could run and play ball.

At fourteen he sat the compulsory school examination. A pass would mean a place at Hemsworth Grammar School but failure would mean a job or the dole queue. Unfortunately there were no test papers for sport and consequently he was left free to seek employment.   He was not upset at the prospect.

Chapter Four

INTO WORK

Charlie's options with regard to work were limited. The alternatives were either the wood-yard or the pit and a relatively uncomplicated working life as a collier.

At the beginning of the second world war the pits were owned by various companies with thousands of directorships. The companies owned two thousand mines and employed over seven hundred thousand men. The mines improved between the wars but the technical standards could not compete with those in the USA or Germany. It was thought that Britain lagged behind in the question of mechanisation because there had been a marked reluctance by the management to spend money on an asset, which the writing on the wall decreed would end up in the hands of the Government.

Within weeks of the outbreak of war there was a great shortage of miners. In the first three weeks twenty-three thousand miners followed the example of their fathers and enlisted. The Government had demanded an increase in production from two hundred and sixty to two hundred and seventy million tonnes per year, but output fell sharply between 1939 and 1942. The attempted joint control of the pits proved ineffective, since although policy was dictated by the Government, the pit manager remained an employee of the owner. As production fell absenteeism increased, something which the public blamed for all the ills in the pits. The President of the

Yorkshire pits at the time dealt with the question extremely well when he said, "A man must be perfectly fit when going down the pit. Ours is an industry where nature has never been kind to us and never will be. Impeded production can occur because of many things, bad roadways and ventilation and our men have to suffer these continued abnormalities and excessive pressures."

Barnsley was one of the oldest coalfields in the country, but the pits were ill-equipped to cope with a wartime economy owing to the shortage of investment in the 1930's.

The demand for more coal during the war years prompted Ernest Bevin, the Minister of Labour at the time, to spend twenty thousand pounds on advertising in 1943 to encourage workers to join the pits. Three thousand men responded, volunteering their services, but the Government were disappointed with this response and introduced conscription with one out of ten men being directed to the mines instead of the armed forces. They were soon to be named 'the Bevin Boys'.

The General Election of 1945 placed the Labour Party in power. In January 1947 nationalisation of the mining industry took effect and within four weeks the country was hit by a disastrous fuel shortage. They were difficult times because more than a million men were out of work because factories had had to close and at the same time the public turned on the miners. It was unfair because there was a shortage of miners, a shortage of coal and a shortage of railway wagons coupled with the worst weather for years. There was a famine of coal in 1947 which turned into a glut four years later and Charlie was to witness higher productivity brought about by mechanisation so that to some extent the miners prospered. There were more pithead baths and even more mobile x-ray units and by the mid-1950's face workers were earning twenty pounds a week.

The increase in prosperity for the mining community meant that miners were buying their own homes, and cars were no longer a middle-class symbol. The hitherto traditional close-knit mining community where everyone knew everyone else and where leisure and pastimes were centred on the street with work being close by were changing. The higher disposable incomes, the motor cars, TVs and holidays abroad did more over the next three decades to destroy the old spirit in the villages than anything else.

On the industrial front, Yorkshire was plagued with unofficial strikes, often being caused by friction with deputies who faced the confrontations on the coal face. Nevertheless during Charlie's time in the mines these changes were in the future and he admits that the increased income had to go hand in hand with that peculiar word called progress.

The pit could be a very dangerous place with accidents occurring on a regular basis and Charlie witnessed the bravery of the miners and particularly the rescue teams, who were called into action when there had been an accident. There are stories of heroism with men pulling at fallen debris with their bare hands when roofs had collapsed and trapped men at the coal face. It is likely that these traumas sealed a special bond and friendship between the miners and Charlie always remembered being able to rely upon his friends in the time of need.

"You had a duty to help your mates and they to help you and it was never more apparent than when there were accidents. Miners were the salt of the earth, treating each other like brothers, always willing to help and support each other."

Charlie was lucky, he had many friends and luckily for him his best friend Gordon Beecher worked at the same colliery; they would walk together to Monkton Pit for they worked the same shifts with Gordon on the pit top and Charlie underground.

Charlie was remarkably unscathed by the mines and the only accident he can recall sustaining was when he trod on a spade which shot up and hit him in the face and somewhere else.

The most feared of all events in the mines were explosions which brought about the release of gas and also the collapsing of roofs so that it was not a place for the claustrophobic or faint-hearted. The sound of an explosion instilled fear into all the miners, and although the lack of air or having to drink pints of water because of the heat were unpleasant impediments, explosions meant accidents, injury and death. It was something that the miner had to live with on each and every shift, on each and every day. The prospect of danger was always with them.

The Government of the day ordered an increase in production and the miner was required to do that little bit extra so the quotas would increase and the more coal that was produced, the more was demanded. Despite the camaraderie and all the pit had to offer, Charlie realised that his future was not in the mines. Inevitably, the problem was where should he go and what should he do since he had no other skill to turn to and there was no other work on offer.

His father had taken a light job on the pit top and Charlie, like all the work force, had been promised that the pits would last for over a hundred years.   Like those who were to follow them, they were misled.   There was little to enjoy with the dirt and the inhuman conditions dominating the working day and the only saving grace was the pay which was better than that to be had at the wood-yard.

His first job at the Monkton Colliery was leading the pit ponies with their harnesses attached to tubs of coal;   a dangerous job which often caught the unwary with their fingers in the couplings of the tubs and it was not uncommon for some of the pit lads to lose the tops of fingers.   The work was based on a two shift system and he would be at work for 5.30am on the morning shift commencing with a thirty minute 'riding time' for travelling to the coal face, followed by work from 6am until 2pm.   This shift would start on Monday and finish at 12 noon on Saturday.   Every day the miners had to face the disagreeable sensation of the cage, for the transportation down the shaft to get to the coal face, when moving at a terrifying rate had the effect of leaving one's stomach at the top whilst the rest travelled downwards at breakneck speed.

The following week would be the afternoon shift with 'riding time' from 1.30pm to 2pm and then a 2pm - 9pm shift before the thirty minute journey back to the pit top. The miners would usually be working in five to six feet high seams which would allow them to stand and work with pick and shovel but there would often be smaller seams where the men had to work on their knees in wet and filthy conditions. Small wonder that emphysema would be one of the predominant legacies of coal-working life endured without sanitation, or running water and in poor lighting. His first wage was twelve shillings and sixpence, in 'old money'. During the early part of the 1940's, Charles' health worsened and he spent more and more time in bed. Charlie worked at the pit during the day and spent the evenings looking after his father.

These were the war years and Charlie remembered standing on the street corner with his friends at night, watching the flashes of light and the sound of distant explosions as the Nazi bombs fell upon a beleaguered Sheffield. The wireless was the entertainment centre of the home and Charlie was an avid listener, particularly to the singers and comedians of the day.

There was much of mining life which Charlie enjoyed and he believes that his fondness for animals came from his work with the pit ponies. In 1947 there were seventy-four thousand ponies at work in the country's mines where in the main they were well treated, apart from the unpleasantness of the conditions in which they worked and the hours spent doing it. It was not unusual for some miners to take hot tea and water down the mine and in some cases the tea was for the pony and the water for the miner. There were instances of extreme kindness and Charlie remembered one occasion where there was a fire and one pony had been left down the pit in the danger zone. One of the miners went back to collect it and insisted that the pony be allowed to enter the cage with the men, refusing to accept that there was insufficient room for them all.

It was remarkable that despite their daily work in very dark conditions, the ponies were extremely nimble footed and when miners were stumbling over every obstacle in their paths, the ponies would tread between the obstructions and miss the lot. It was not unusual for miners to share their 'snap' with the ponies and many took extra food to give them. The 'snap tin' was of metal construction so that it was not unknown to see teeth marks around the rims, where the ponies had lost patience in waiting for their share.

One of the golden rules in the pit was that no-one should ride the ponies but it was a rule which was not always observed. Charlie was a would-be 'lone ranger' and he liked nothing more than to ride his favourite pony along the tracks to the coal face. It was an enterprise which was enjoyed by both pony and rider, although it was an offence punishable by a fine if you were caught.

Charlie enjoyed his daily ride but the deputies were crafty as they knew that the miners were breaking the rules, so they would place men at certain intervals in discreet alcoves where they could not be seen. As the ponies rode past they would flick whitewash at horse and rider and when the managers made their inspections, they would be able to find the offenders by observing the forensic evidence.

Despite the dangers, there were always workers who liked to enjoy a joke and Charlie, like some of his colleagues, was a prankster. One old dodge was to hook buckets of water to the ceilings and attach them to string. The trick was to wait until colleagues were walking underneath the bucket and then to tilt it by pulling the string, so that they were administered an unwanted shower.

On one occasion he decided that he would give two of his mates a soaking and so he clinically prepared a bucket by filling it with water and adding some gifts left by the ponies to the mixture, then laid in wait until he heard voices and believing it was his two work-mates, made ready to spring the surprise. As they walked underneath the bucket he pulled the string, and the water and other contents of a more unpleasant nature were tipped onto the unsuspecting walkers. Unfortunately it happened to be one of the managers and his deputy who were on an inspection.

"Fortunately my colour saved me that day, as I managed to sneak by without them seeing me. I always said being black was a massive advantage at times."

There was one incident which occurred in one of the local pits when two lads actually fell asleep in one of the roadways, which was a serious offence and was punishable by a heavy fine. A new manager had taken over by the name of Len Parkin (the father of the famous newscaster and television personality Leonard Parkin), and he was carrying out an inspection when he came across the slumbering youths. He poked them with his stick and asked them if they knew who he was. Charlie's sure that the old joke came from that incident when one of the miners replied, "Well if tha dunt know, what chance 'ave I got?" They were both fined and censured.

Charles eventually retired from work and spent the majority of his time at home but his health was failing and he ceased to be able to look after himself.

Consequently he was taken to the Hemsworth Hospital, also known as the 'workhouse'. It was a considerable trauma for both father and son as Charlie stood by powerless to help his ailing father to whom he was so devoted. Charlie believed that his father was indestructible, largely because he had always been there and had been such a commanding figure, a giant of a man, but despite all his qualities he was a mere mortal and in 1944 just after Charlie's sixteenth birthday, Charles Augustus died.

Charlie was distraught as his guiding light, father and best friend had gone. He speaks easily and with great pride of his father, and the single-handed way in which he had been brought up. The old man had never learned to read or write, but his son was a source of constant pride for his relatively limited educational achievement. He had protected his son from the tragedy of prejudice, providing a legacy of fortitude resilience and an indomitable spirit.

Fortunately Charlie was not alone and he left South Hiendley to live at Upton near Pontefract and enjoy the solace of the family atmosphere with his aunt Edith Bedford. A transfer to Upton Colliery was quickly arranged and the working cycle continued from the morning shift to afternoons and so on and so forth. Whilst he disliked the work, he enjoyed mixing with his fellow miners, recalling them as a 'witty crew' with whom he enjoyed the repartee of the workplace. But there were risks to health and of accidental injury and not so accidental injury if your face did not fit.

Life with the Bedford family was happy and supportive, although memories of his father and his teachings remained with him. There were four sons Dennis, George, Ralph and Gerald, all of whom were good athletes and Charlie formed an alliance born out of a common interest in sport which was to help him to form the basis of his footballing career.

His family were the only black people in the area. They may not have been blood relatives, but being a minority there was a common bond and everyone became an uncle, aunt or cousin in the form of an extended family. He remembers fondly how black people would always speak to each other in passing, no doubt because there were so few around, a considerable contrast with today when the level of camaraderie seems to have diminished with the increasing number of immigrants.

The Bedfords lived in a four-bedroomed colliery house where Charlie shared a bedroom with Gerald and he remained with them until his marriage in 1957. He was fortunate, there was a bathroom, but the toilet was outside and had no lock.

"You had to be a good singer, especially if you were delayed in the lavatory. Over the years I taught myself a good many songs!"

Youth clubs were booming with the objective of persuading children away from street corners. They had a number of facilities, certainly more than were available at home and Charlie enjoyed the spirit of friendship which prevailed. Cinema was also an attraction with weekly visits to the Upton or South Elmsall picture palaces and an occasional visit to the Barnsley cinema took him to the infamous 'Bugs Hut' apparently so aptly named. Charlie remembered it well.

"You left with a smile on your face and a rash on your arse."

Athletics was ever popular and as a hobby it was free, with the only expense being the kit to run in. There were meetings every weekend and of course Yorkshire provided some of the best athletes of the day. It was an honest and entertaining endeavour and Charlie showed great promise in which his strength was his speed; something which he was to put to good use during his football career.

The prosperity of the village depended upon the colliery, consequently the majority of the working men on the street walked the same path to the pit and so there was always someone to travel and clock in with. Despite the benefits of convenience and camaraderie Charlie was desperately keen to get out of the mines and his sporting prowess was to prove the vehicle with which to do it.

His spare time was spent on the football fields around his home and in the evenings when he was old enough and when finance permitted, he visited the local workingmen's clubs in search of entertainment. Charlie would sit and watch the performers as they plied their trade, enjoying the singers and particularly the comedians, with whom he felt an affinity. His gift of an excellent memory allowed him to recount the jokes he had heard to his pals, when he was back at work in the pit, so that in time he built up a considerable repertoire. In those early days the wages at the pit were poor and after all the dues and demands had been paid there was very little left over for entertainment. Charlie was inventive and always had his eye on the main chance, and together with Ike and Gordon Beecher he would make regular visits to the Friendship Inn at Gawber near Barnsley, where a talent night was held on Fridays. Volunteers were taken onto the stage to perform their act, whether it be a song or a monologue or even jokes. Charlie would get up and sing one of the popular songs of the day and if his luck was in he would win, and there would be a cash prize which would provide the beer money for the evening.

Ike and Gordon place a rather interesting slant upon Charlie's career because they never expected that he would become a famous comedian. They, like many, thought that his forte was in singing, but they were never happier than when they could sit and watch Charlie perform.

The Workingmen's Clubs were the heart of the community's entertainment long before the ownership of televisions became commonplace and in those days they were unlike the clubs of today. It is true that they didn't have the sophisticated sound and lighting equipment of the modern day, but they did have audiences who were prepared to listen and not compete with the performers. The concert secretary signalled the start of an act by switching off the lights in the auditorium and the ringing of his bell. Not a sound would be heard during the performance and certainly no-one would walk to the bar or show the artist any lack of consideration during the performance. How things have changed. Television and radio broadcasts have brought entertainment to a wider audience and have made variety common-place. Audiences have changed too, but in those days they went to the clubs for the entertainment and the company, not the chance of cheap beer and bingo. Saturday afternoons were reserved for football and Charlie soon came to the notice of the local colliery football team manager, who signed him to play for them in a league which was not for the faint-hearted. The ubiquitous football scout trawled the local leagues in search of talent for the higher echelons of the football hierarchy and Charlie was to attract one or two of them who, despite his age, kept very substantial notes about the coloured kid from Ryhill. He was five feet eleven and a gangly youth, but someone who showed an early but considerable promise.

When he was nineteen years old Leeds United invited him to play as an amateur in his favourite position at centre-half. By his own admission, Charlie did not have the gift of great skill, but he was extremely fit and had a turn of speed which more than made up for the other so-called deficiencies. He was also eleven-and-a-half stone of muscle and bone with a surfeit of courage.

It was an era however where he was to taste the perennial bitterness of racism and it would never be more apparent than at the weekends when he went out with some of his friends from the colliery. He was extremely popular and often entertained them in lighter moments with a song and a never-ending fund of stories and jokes. Not all the people in the area however were attracted to this likeable coloured lad with the broad Yorkshire accent.

A regular calling place was Gordon Beecher's house, who by that time had married his wife Iris. Charlie had built up a great friendship with Iris whom he refers to affectionately as 'Ike' and to this day still respects her views and advice.

When he was in his teens and early twenties he would take his girlfriends to visit Ike's house. There were two reasons, the first of which was that there was nowhere else to go, for there was little money for entertainment, and secondly he always appreciated Ike's opinion. She recalls those days with great affection,

"It was not unusual for Charlie to visit us on a Sunday morning for he was always an early riser, and he would let himself in and light the fire, make some tea and bring it up to our room. I would always shout at him for waking me up so early, but he would just laugh and tell me there was no point 'ligging' in bed on a rest day! He would always come back on a Saturday night after he'd been out with his girlfriend and would promptly go to the cooker and cook everybody liver and onions, which was his favourite meal. He rather fancied himself as a chef, but only so far as liver and onions were concerned."

On 'Dame Night' at the clubs, Charlie would often feel the eyes of other men upon him when he danced with a white girl and he had to endure the backlash of nasty and offensive remarks. He particularly remembers such comments to the girls as 'if you go with him, you will go with owt'. Fortunately he had the support of his friends and some of the girls would not be intimidated by such remarks, so Charlie was not isolated. He remembers one hurtful incident when a young lady, with whom he was friendly, broke off their association because her father had found them out and had ordered that it was to stop. He simply told her not to go against her father's wishes as it would only cause her trouble. Charlie felt that her father believed he was acting in her best interests but the rebuff really hurt. Charlie had learned tolerance which had given him an unusual insight into the strange dispositions of people. It was not an acceptance of inferiority, but a recognition of ignorance in others.

What made matters worse was that he was a half-caste. Prejudice came from all angles, but was never more upsetting than when full-blooded Africans would look down upon him because he was part white.

It was more noticeable in public places and particularly in pubs where customers would often nudge each other and nod in his direction. He remembers occasions when there would be whispering and he would know it was aimed in his direction, and then one of the misguided group would boldly walk up to him and ask, "Are you enjoying yourself in England?" They would always be shocked when he replied in his Yorkshire accent, "I certainly am, my old love."

He would often be taken for a student and when questioned he would say that he was studying medicine, because that's what people believed the 'majority of coloured men did'. "It was easier that way," Charlie would say.

If there was ever trouble, his friends would stand in his corner, although Charlie would prefer not to fight, remembering the words of his father when he advised that it would only mean the purchase of a new suit.

It is a peculiar thing about race for it engenders the extremes of loyalty and dislike, something exemplified by a story from Ike Beecher.

A favourite holiday haunt was Blackpool and for three or four days each year Mr & Mrs Beecher would stay in a boarding house accompanied more often than not by Charlie, who to avoid embarrassment insisted that Ike enquire when the booking was made that no exception would be taken to his colour. It is remarkable to think that such an indignity was imposed by reason of the colour of a person's skin.

If Charlie needed another ally he had it in his size, fitness and strength and if the necessity arose he was well able to look after himself. But he was also gifted with a degree of common sense and insight and cold steel determination which he would put to good use throughout the rest of his life. His ambition was to leave the pit and the only way this could be achieved was to pursue a career in football, so he spent approximately four months with Leeds United and felt that he was good enough to attract professional terms, but unfortunately because there was a shortage of money in football, amateur terms were preferred by Leeds to save on the wages bill. Charlie chose to leave, returning to his beloved Upton Colliery team, but the scouts who had spied upon him in his middle teens were to return with offers more tempting than those of Leeds United.

Ray Singleton played in one of the colliery teams and remembered Charlie from more than one confrontation:

"He would kick you to death and then laugh. He was a good sportsman and never bore a grudge, but then he was not usually the one injured. He had a nice way with him and would often sit with you telling jokes as the physio tried to help you walk again."

Following excellent reports about his playing, he was offered trials at Notts County, York City and Doncaster Rovers and could have signed for either club, but his preference was for the Rovers and the 1947/48 season saw him playing in the reserves. It was not long before he signed as a semi-professional.

Subsequently he was offered fully professional terms and an end to his life in the mines accompanied by no regrets at leaving. His first wage as a professional player was twenty pounds per week, but the most important thing was that he was doing something that he loved. He was young, keen and able, with a future at his feet but he was also a pathfinder because there were few if any black players in the football league, and so Charlie was a standard bearer who took his responsibilities very seriously. Once again and not for the last time, Charlie had something to prove. He was up to the task. He believed it represented his destiny. His future was in football, he had considered nothing else.

As Charlie began his football career, on 22 June 1948 the ship *Empire Windrush* steamed into Tilbury Docks amidst a thick fog, making its way up the Thames until it reached its mooring. The ship was carrying a number of Caribbean immigrants, some of the first to make their home in this country and they were the first of many. The tabloids had already begun to engender an anti-immigrant feeling, which extended itself to Parliament where one M.P. was alleged to have said that the first English winter would put paid to any desires that they might have had to stay. But they stayed on, facing an ever-growing resentment based on racial ignorance. Charlie had an advantage because he had been born here and he knew all about the British winters.

It was a peculiar state of affairs, but the more immigrants that arrived, the greater the prejudice, and the greater the fear.

Chapter Five

DONCASTER ROVERS

C harlie was a natural centre-half of the 'old school' being just under six feet tall and weighing in at eleven-and-a-half stone. He was good in the air, extremely quick on the ground and was seen as the replacement in waiting for Bill Pattison, the Scottish International, who was being groomed for a transfer to Newcastle United. But Charlie had to wait for his chance.

In the 1949/50 football season, Doncaster Rovers were in League Division 3 North and the ground capacity at Belle Vue was forty-four thousand, although it rarely ever achieved figures of over twenty-three thousand. The average attendance per home game was just short of eighteen thousand - a far cry from the obscurity of the Vauxhall Conference League when Doncaster lost its football league status at the end of the 1997/98 season.

Belle Vue had been the home ground of the Rovers since election to the Football League on the 4th September 1901, although the club had a chequered history, losing its place in the Football League until it was re-elected in 1923.

The 1949/50 season saw Charlie's arrival and also promotion to the then Division II where the club was to enjoy the next nine seasons, only to be relegated to Division Three in 1957/58.

Charlie was around at a time when football was not only popular but was the staple diet of the sporting masses, as exemplified by average attendances at the time of about twenty thousand from 1949/50 to 1951/52 and thirteen thousand from then to 1957/58. It was an era where football was *the* sport and support for the Rovers has not been exceeded since.

Charlie started in the reserves, being promoted to the first team in 1953 where he was to become one of the most popular players ever to play at Belle Vue. He enjoyed the training, the playing and the support of some wonderful fans.

He was signed by Jackie Bestall, the Rovers manager and former England International who at that time had a squad of forty players on his books to choose from; a situation which no longer exists even with the biggest of clubs. The maximum wage for footballers was an arrangement which was to remain unchanged until 1960, and so in those days clubs could afford a larger workforce.

Once again Charlie was one of a minority. He was one of only a handful of black players around at the time and not for the first time, young Williams was breaking new ground, a forerunner of so many of the talented black players in the league today.

His apprenticeship was far from easy as competition was rife, with Charlie vying for position with the club centre-half and hero of the day Syd Bycroft, who had occupied that position for over twenty years. Many a talented player had grown old waiting in the wings for Bycroft to retire.

In 1950 Bestall moved on and was replaced by Peter Doherty the legendary Silver Fox, a former Northern Ireland International who came to Rovers as player-manager.   Doherty was a great player who was revered by the entire playing staff, and used his consummate skill and considerable presence to guide Rovers to great success.   He was a very able coach and took time to help Charlie along a path fraught with fierce competition, to a place in the first team.   What Charlie lost in skill he more than made up for with endeavour, which gave him many admirers amongst the faithful supporters at Belle Vue.

Initially Charlie was a stalwart of the reserve team and the 1950/51 season saw him replace the great Byford, after Rovers worst defensive season which had conceded ninety-five goals in forty-two matches.

Charlie warmed to his work and his first season in the first team saw him play in 40 matches.   Thereafter he was ever-present apart from injuries when he earned the reputation as being one of the hardest players in the league.

The formation in those days was two full-backs, two wing-halves, the centre-half and five forwards.   Four four two, four three three and the rest had not arrived in the coaching manual and the role of centre-half had one real purpose, namely to stop the other side scoring; something at which Charlie was more than adept.   He thrilled the crowds with his passionate play and inspiring courage.   He would never flinch from a tackle and would not balk at a challenge when it presented itself to him. He said of his defensive role, "The ball might have gone past me, and sometimes the player, but never both at the same time."   The result was that Charlie became the scourge of opposing centre-forwards.

One such player was the renowned Brian Clough who was playing for Middlesborough and Charlie's job was to mark him out of the game. Clough was carving out a career as a goal scorer, something which was to eventually bring him to the attention of the England manager of the day, Walter Winterbottom, and a string of England caps.

In one match, Charlie had played Clough out of the game. Everywhere Clough went Charlie followed and when the half-time whistle went they walked off the pitch together prompting a verbal exchange.

"You'll not be able to follow me into the dressing-room as well," snapped Clough.

"No," replied Charlie, "But I'll be out 'ere waiting for thee when tha comes out!"

They played against each other many times but Charlie cannot remember Cloughy scoring in any of those matches.

Tony Bluff is the club historian, a doyen of facts and figures who has painstakingly prepared an archive of statistics over the years and who knows more about Doncaster Rovers than anyone else. He is the co-author with his colleague Barry Watson, of the book 'Dony - the Official History' which catalogues facts and figures too numerous to mention here. Tony began supporting Rovers in the early 1950's and witnessed the rise of Charlie Williams the professional footballer.

"Charlie was one of my favourite players. Whilst he was not the most skilful he was a 'muck or nettles' player. He thrilled the crowds by stopping forwards. He was a hard player and probably if he was playing now he would spend most of his time suspended, but it just didn't happen then. He was not an intentional fouler but he was truly a very hard man who gave no quarter. I liked him because he always gave one hundred per cent, no matter what. I have seen him play through injuries and crunching tackles which would leave some of today's players writhing in agony. It was a man's game then and it suited Charlie."

Charlie trained hard to keep in peak fitness but he also looked after himself, eating properly and leaving alcohol to those who were not in earnest. Consequently he kept his place in the team. He was not only driven by the desire to do well, but also by the over-riding fear of insecurity.

Charlie was not always the hero. He was ever popular with the home fans but when he played at away games he found himself the brunt of the opposing supporters. Some things do not change and once again the greater the endeavour and success, the greater the prejudice and the more vehement the abuse. Tony Bluff noted Charlie's self-discipline.

"He never bit once when the opposing supporters had a go at him. He seemed to take it in his stride. If anything, it made him more determined. I have never before seen a more determined player."

Charlie was happy. He was enjoying himself and once again had found camaraderie amongst the other players and staff. The formula for friendship was the same as existed at the colliery and Charlie made friends with considerable ease.

One player in particular was to become one of Charlie's best friends and a man who in later years was to play a considerable part in his life. Alick Jeffrey was the

Doncaster 'wonder-boy' who signed for Doncaster Rovers when he was just fifteen years old to become one of the most elegant and cultured players the club ever produced. He was exposed to the glare of international honours by being picked to play for the England Under-23 team in 1956, but unfortunately his career was blighted by a broken leg whilst playing for his country.

Alick was playing for the England Under-23 side against France at Bristol when after only ten minutes of play Alick broke a leg. It was a serious injury which brought the curtain down on his international career. He was never the same again.

Just before the England v France game, Alick had discussions with the great Matt Busby of Manchester United who was attempting to sign him. Busby had met with a great deal of resistance from Peter Doherty, the Doncaster manager, so much so that he shelved the idea with a view to resurrecting his interest when Alick's contract had ended. People often suggest to Alick that he was unlucky to have missed this opportunity, but he held a philosophical view of the 'disappointment'. He believes that if he had signed for United, there could be little doubt that he would have played for the 'Busby Babes' in the 1958 season and faced the tragedy of the air crash. He recalls,

"Fate is a funny thing. Who knows what would have happened. I don't consider myself unlucky, quite the reverse, it clearly was not meant for me to join Manchester United."

Alick remembers Mr Busby giving him one hundred pounds in cash after telling him that Peter Doherty had blocked the transfer. It was the equivalent of eight weeks' wages and he will never forget Busby's words when he said,

"Go and buy something nice for your mother and I'll see you another time."

Alick believes Busby to have been the best manager Britain every produced.

Another of Charlie's friends and colleagues was the brilliant Irish goalkeeper Harry Gregg who signed for Doncaster in the 1955/56 season. He too came to the attention of Matt Busby who signed him in 1958 and Gregg was one of the survivors of the crash which killed so many of the great players who made up possibly the greatest team Manchester ever produced.

Charlie would enjoy the dressing-room banter and the 'Three Musketeers' Gregg, Jeffrey and Williams became the club jokers and once again his sense of humour and ability to tell jokes earned him a reputation as a character. Alick Jeffrey was noted for being a prankster and it was not unusual for practical jokes to get out of hand.

"Charlie was always up to some joke or other, playing tricks on his team mates. One day we decided we would get him back. It was winter and it was particularly cold. There had been a heavy snowfall which had turned to sleet and then when the temperatures dipped, it turned to ice. The groundsman had been clearing the ice off the terraces and there was a massive pile outside the dressing-rooms. After training we were having a hot bath when we decided to get a few shovels of ice and surprise Charlie with it. Charlie was standing in the bath, telling someone a joke, when four or five of us came in and let him have the ice from all angles. I had never heard Charlie swear until that day!"

It was not all fun and laughter however because Charlie devoted much of his time to maintaining a high level of fitness and he would often go on long cross-country runs when the other players had gone home to rest. He knew that his strength lay in his speed, coupled with an outstanding mobility, and the only way to ensure that this was maintained was to put in hour after hour and mile after mile of road work, in all weathers and conditions. The worse the weather, the better it was, because it was all part and parcel of the 'hardening-up process'.

Charlie had a good liaison with his manager, Peter Doherty and under his coaching he benefited greatly to become a very effective centre-half. But once again Charlie had something to prove - a feature of his entire life – as a standard bearer for the ethnic minorities for whom he felt a responsibility. It was a complicated situation because being half-caste he was neither one thing nor the other, and was to be discriminated against by both sides. Perhaps the combination of such 'disadvantages' made him all the more determined to succeed since his new vocation brought him greater prosperity and with it the desire to keep it.

In the 1953/54 season Charlie met a girl at a dance with the unlikely name of Audrey Crump and they started courting. The association brought him into contact with Mrs Crump senior who was a likeable and kindly lady and Charlie was accepted as a member of the family. He recalls her with great affection.

"We got on like a house on fire. I was her favourite lad and she couldn't do enough for me, and to some extent she was the mother figure that I never had."

The relationship with Audrey was severely tested, for she was Caucasian and there was considerable antagonism towards mixed relationships but in 1957 Charlie and Audrey were married at the village church at Ryhill in Barnsley. Charlie was twenty-nine years of age, Audrey was twenty and the wedding took place on the first of April. Charlie did not realise it at the time but the date was an omen.

He was playing for the Rovers every Saturday, so a weekend wedding was not possible but a pleasant Monday wedding, with Charlie's cousin, Gerald Bedford, acting as best man enabled the whole team to turn up in support and most of the villagers turned out to watch. There was a reception in the church hall and a party in the local club that evening but no honeymoon because match commitments demanded they wait until the football season was over.

The regular income from the football team allowed Charlie to take on a mortgage and the couple bought a semi-detached house in Doncaster, not far from the racecourse and the football ground. There were problems with the transaction and the keys were not actually delivered for about three months, so Charlie and Audrey moved in with Mrs Crump. Surprisingly enough she was sorry to see them go when three months later Charlie and Audrey moved into their new home during the 1957/58 season when Charlie was enjoying a great spell in the first team.

He was extremely popular with the Belle Vue faithful, but success brought drawbacks as well as rewards. It has long been the case that opposing supporters will barrack the other side's players and will cheer a mistake or a downfall and if it is done in good humour it is acceptable. But sadly there are always those who have to resort to bad behaviour to make their point and Charlie was often the brunt of that unruly element who chose to resort to racist abuse, particularly when he tackled an opposing player roughly. There were no safeguards for black players in those days, probably because they were so few in number and society was not as enlightened as it is now to the cause of prejudice in sport.

Charlie's last season at Doncaster saw him play in twenty-one of the forty-three matches. He had suffered some injuries and consequently had not played with his usual degree of regularity, also he was approaching thirty-two years of age and his electrifying pace had begun to desert him.

"It was the time in my career that I feared more than anything else. I knew that I couldn't go on for ever, but I kept believing that I had another season, because it's very difficult for a professional footballer to come to terms with age. After all, it was my chosen career. When that was finished so was I, or so I thought. Consequently I didn't want to go."

Charlie had played almost twelve seasons of good quality football, and as a senior player he was entitled to a Testimonial, the proceeds being paid gross because there was no tax liability on such sums. However there were problems within the board of directors and Doncaster faced relegation for the first time in many years. The politics of the boardroom put paid to any hopes Charlie had of a nest egg but instead he did receive two benefits. The first was with the reserve team which brought him £350 gross, leaving him with £240 after tax and the second with the first team which raised £750 out of which he received £504 net so that after ten years of loyal service, he received less than £1,000.

Charlie discussed his situation with the Board and it became clear that Doncaster had decided to place him on the transfer list, but because of the financial position that they were in at the time, they had placed a £3,500 transfer fee against his name.   This was a substantial sum in those days, especially for a thirty-two year old with dodgy knees. Charlie was upset that he did not have a testimonial, and the least he expected in those circumstances was a free transfer.   There can be no doubt that he deserved better, but it was not to be and consequently Charlie was left to make some very important decisions which were to end an otherwise illustrious career with the South Yorkshire Club and the Football League.

Chapter Six

SHOWBUSINESS BECKONS

Comedy is a special talent with a sense of timing the main ingredient.

Charlie had such a talent and he tried out his skills most successfully both at the pit and in the changing rooms of one hundred football teams. He was 'one of the lads' and his friendship with his working and playing colleagues was another integral factor, but he never overlooked the discrimination he had to endure. He felt that it made him all the more determined.

Ever since childhood, Charlie had the ability to make people laugh with that intrinsic quality of timing and his endearing personality. He delighted in making friends, and of course friendship removed prejudice.

Charlie worked at his relationships at a natural and genuine level invoking passionate loyalty in others and wherever he went more and more people were added to his ever-growing list of supporters. He was enjoying his football and was earning an impressive reputation, but it also left him time to extend his interests into other areas.

It was his old friend Alick Jeffrey who introduced Charlie to the stage. It wasn't a skilfully conceived plan but one of those things that just happened, and little did he know then how it was to change the course of his future.

Alick's father was a singer in the local clubs, and with his show-business background Alick junior learned about music. He would entertain his friends accompanying his pleasant singing voice on the guitar, leading many people to suggest a career in show-business when his playing days were over. Charlie would often join in having an above average singing voice which he put to good use forming a double act with Alick to entertain the rest of the team.

One of the other players suggested they form an act and as a result Mr Jeffrey senior was co-opted into the group and the Jeffrey Trio was formed.

It was a humble beginning, but they began rehearsing at 'after match gatherings' providing entertainment for the players and their friends, but eventually they were offered their first semi-professional engagement at a pub in Armthorpe, Doncaster entertaining members of the supporters' club. They were well received, doubtless trading upon their popularity as players, but people noticed that Charlie had a little more than the average amount of talent.

It wasn't long before they were playing at other Doncaster Rovers Supporters' Club functions, having at first only sufficient material for one spot, but eventually this was extended by adding extra songs to the repertoire with the odd joke thrown in between.

It was unusual for a coloured man with a strong Yorkshire accent to tell jokes, and there can be no doubt that for the first time Charlie saw his colour as a possible advantage. Charlie Williams the semi-professional comedian was born.

Jeffrey remembers their act,

"Charlie was a good singer in the 'crooner' style. I knew he was a bit of a joker, but I never really thought he would become a comedian. It wasn't until I came back from Australia when Charlie had been solo for a time, that I noticed the accent on comedy. Not only that, he was good!"

He was wise enough to know that his audience acceptance was based upon his position in the Club, but others suggested that the act had prospects and so they persevered, firstly with some new songs and secondly with more humour to break up the musical part of the act. The Jeffrey Trio became the toast of the local Supporters' Clubs.

Charlie fancied himself as a singer and had not considered comedy.

"There were no black comics and to be honest I never really considered it." He had studied performers in the local club scene and he had based his presentation upon what he had seen and heard. There was a nucleus of popular songs which were doing the rounds rather like they do today and he knew which were tried and tested, and consequently he would often call upon the audience to join in. The songs were taken from the hit parade of the day and most people seemed to know the words and the tendency of the club-going public was to sing along. The most interesting thing was the peculiar phenomenon of audiences laughing out loud when Charlie walked on stage and greeted everyone in a broad Yorkshire accent.

His famous catchphrase, "Good evening my flowers" was born one night at a club in Bessacar near Doncaster. He had taken the term of endearment "My old flower", fairly common in parts of Barnsley, and tailored its use to suit his own greeting. It was to remain with him for the rest of his career.

The tendency to 'milk' a good thing took the form of adding the odd comment or two to his introduction by focusing upon his accent and before anyone could use the point to heckle or insult, he would refer to his 'suntan'. The use of self-criticism broke down any barriers and stopped anyone else from claiming the privilege, leaving the joke on him or at least that's what the audience thought.

"The first task was to catch their attention, then the real test was to keep it."

Charlie certainly gained their attention for there were no black comics around, certainly so far as the north of England was concerned, and with their interest stimulated he would begin to speak in his strong Yorkshire accent.

Sydney Wort, who writes under the pseudonym of Yardov Hale for the periodical *'The Clubman's Guide'* was a devotee of the local clubland scene. He recalled the charm and indeed novelty of the Jeffrey Trio.

"They were a popular act which concentrated upon songs from the hit parade of the day and with a black singer, they were a novelty."

But it was not until Charlie embarked upon a solo career that he put the novelty value to good use.

Chapter Seven

SKEGNESS TOWN

In 1959 and at 32 years of age Charlie's professional footballing career was coming to an end after match appearances over a period of eleven years. The transfer fee on his name was a substantial sum in those days, particularly for someone of his age with problematical knees and so Charlie the realist took over. He saw little point in sitting on the subs bench waiting for the offer that may never come and so he accepted an invitation to meet representatives of Skegness Town F.C.

It was understandable that Charlie was disappointed by the actions of the Doncaster board of directors, for the transfer fee was much more than any club was likely to want to pay. The effect was to limit Charlie's prospects of continuing to play in the Football League so that he was staring reserve team and possible 'A' team football in the face, neither of which prospects appealed to him.

Fortunately fate was to lend a hand again and it did so in the form of his old friend Alick Jeffrey. Alick's broken leg whilst playing for England had brought down the curtain on his league career, certainly at that time. Nevertheless he had managed to secure a position with the Midland League team, Skegness Town, where he was enjoying a new lease of life. He had kept in constant touch with Charlie, knew about the difficulties at the Rovers and suggested to the club that Charlie would make an ideal acquisition. Skegness Town were ambitious and had managed to secure the services of the late George Rayner as manager who had enjoyed great success in the football world. He had managed the Swedish national team throughout the 1958 World Cup campaign, seeing them into the final itself against the great Brazilian side which included a little known seventeen year old youngster who was to glory in the golden name of Pele.

Mr Rayner had returned to England and accepted the offer of the Skegness board and when Alick Jeffrey became available Mr Rayner seized his opportunity and signed him. It was a sound addition to club strength because Alick was a very good player, and but for the injury, had been destined for great things. There can be no doubt that he was to be a considerable asset in the Midland League.

Mr Rayner knew all about Charlie's capabilities and after one meeting in 1959 he offered him a contract which was worth fifteen pounds a week; some five pounds less than at Doncaster, but with the added incentive of a house at a subsidised rent and a job outside of the football club, he had equalled his former salary. At Doncaster he was training four times a week with a match on Saturdays and the odd mid-week fixture. He was formerly earning twenty pounds a week but in the last analysis, the deal at Skegness was far more attractive, with his services being claimed for only two days a week training with a match each Saturday. He was able to take a part-time job as non-league football did not make the demands upon its players as did the professional league, and a job was found for him by the Club President as a driver delivering Skegness rock (of the confectionery kind) for a local firm called Haywards.

This arrangement suited his training requirements and paid him ten pounds a week. He had progressed from a terraced house in South Hiendley to a semi-detached property in a pleasant area of Skegness. It was a sensible move and extended Charlie's playing career with a number of old colleagues, especially his own friend Alick Jeffrey.

Charlie had enjoyed a 'purple patch' and was made club captain. Mick French was a player in the side at that time, playing on the left wing, but is now the club historian and remembers Charlie's training regime.

"He was extremely fit and very, very quick. He was also one of the hardest players around but even so he was never dirty, although I suppose it might have seemed like it to opposing players.

"I used to train with him and Alick Jeffrey and when Alick and I had finished, Charlie would go on a cross-country run just for the hell of it before calling us all sorts of names for being idle!"

The second season saw Skegness at the top of the league and promotion so that Charlie was enjoying his football and the sea air, and there was always the bonus of as much free mint rock as he could eat.

Charlie became very popular with the Skegness faithful and his sense of humour and his singing expertise enhanced his reputation. The local newspapers followed his career quite closely, causing one of them to feature him in a special article called the 'Sportrait'.

Singing Footballer Likes a Laugh

'The visiting team is attacking strongly. Then the ball is cleared and somebody shouts. "Good old Charlie" and Charlie Williams, popular centre-half and captain of Skegness Town, urges the Lilywhites into the counter-attack.

'Not always however, does that cry mean that Charlie Williams has broken up an attack. Quite often it indicates that he has livened up a dull game with a bit of clowning, for he is undisputedly the comedian of Burgh Road.

'Mind you, he never allows a little fun to spoil his game. "It's just that I see the funny side of things so easily," he told a *'Standard'* reporter. "I have a good sense of humour and I like a laugh on the field. I live for the game and enjoy every match. When I shout at other players it's simply because I get carried away with enthusiasm. We are forever making mistakes and forever learning from them."

'Now approaching his thirtieth birthday, Charlie was born at Royston near Barnsley and is the son of British West Indians who emigrated from Barbados. He was brought up at Upton, near Doncaster, and it was there that his junior footballing days were spent. After a year with the local colliery side he was spotted by Leeds Untied and joined them as an eighteen year old amateur.

'Keen to become a professional, he found that his chances of doing so with Leeds were not so good, and a year later in 1948 he returned to Upton. Before long however, he was back with a professional club, this time Doncaster Rovers, with whom he was to stay for the next ten years until he joined Skegness Town.

'In the reserves as a part-time professional he became a utility player at half-back, forward, full-back, in fact everywhere but goal, and for three seasons he captained the Midland League side.

'His determination was rewarded late in 1955 when manager Doherty surprised him with the news, "You are selected at centre-half against Plymouth tomorrow."

'Soon after his return to the first team came one of the most remarkable F.A. Cup series in the history of the competition. It started with a fourth round 0-0 draw against Aston Villa and continued its marathon run with a 2-2 draw at Villa Park, a 1-1 draw at Manchester, another goal-less draw at Sheffield, and finally, a 3-1 triumph at West Bromwich.

'In that memorable game, Alick Jeffrey scored two of the Doncaster goals. Charlie has known him since he joined Doncaster as a fifteen year old on the ground staff (he was sixteen when he helped in the Villa defeat), and for five years they have been great pals. "Those five cup games were really gruelling because they were all played on heavy grounds. Three days later we met Birmingham in the fifth round. They won 2-1 but were the luckiest team alive!"

'The sixty thousand crowd for that match was the biggest Charlie played before. "The atmosphere was electric, but it was a great feeling," he said.

'For the next three years he was a regular choice for the first team (relegated to Division Three in 1958) and in Division Two and F.A. Cup games he played against many of today's international players, including the great John Charles.

'Charlie then came to Skegness. Why Skegness? "I thought they had done pretty well in their first Midland League season, and it seemed a nice little club with ambition and enthusiasm. I like Skegness - it's healthy, and the people are friendly. I'm well satisfied and would only go back to the Football League with a Division Two club. Even then I would not easily be drawn back," he added.

'He is employed by Messrs A Haywood and Sons, the Cavendish Road rock manufacturers.

'Singing is Charlie's main interest outside football. When Skegness met Grantham in the F.A. Cup, the day he was first made captain, he was due to compete in the final of a talent competition at Middleton Towers, near Morecambe, where he, his wife Audrey, and their two year old son Melford spent their holiday this year.

'At Doncaster he sang in a vocal group known as the Jeffrey Trio with Alick and his father. They became very popular in the Sheffield and Barnsley districts, singing at socials and charity concerts.

'Since meeting again at Skegness - they are neighbours in Church Lane, Winthorpe - Charlie and Alick have renewed their singing activities and on Sunday entertain at the Workingmen's Club, Cleethorpes.

'But football is his life, and to the young lads who have enough promise to become professionals, (there are one or two in Skegness), Charlie offers this advice, "He must remember if he wants to make the grade that there is no substitute for hard work. He is not kidding anybody if he doesn't do his training. He only kids himself."'

In 1960 Alick was given the opportunity of finishing his career in Australia. Sydney Football Club were anxious to improve their style and quality of play and there was no better way to do it than to trawl the English league for players who were either at or about retirement but who would still be able to do a good job in the somewhat lower standards of the Australian league. Alick seized his chance with both hands and signed a two year contract, and in February 1960 he embarked on the twelve thousand mile journey to what he thought would be the final stage of his footballing career.

Charlie remained at Skegness for a further season, but the rigours of competitive football at that level meant that the injuries took a little longer to recover from. His once electric pace was now waning and whilst still welcome at the club, Charlie knew that the writing was on the wall and the old insecurities visited him again. There is little or no sentiment in football and understandably when one's usefulness had been exhausted, there was little else left but to move down a league, accompanied of course by an appropriate drop in salary.

The terms of the contract were negotiated by Charlie direct with the club. There were no high-flying agents or intermediaries claiming a percentage. Sponsorship and the complicated financial strategies surrounding football in the 1990's were not even on the accountant's drawing board in those days as the sport itself was the first consideration and not the ramifications of the share index. When asked if he would like to have played in modern day football, Charlie smiles and pauses before answering, "I would have liked their wages," he says earnestly.

But the differences did not just extend to matters of money. Charlie played at a time when you needed to wear a crash-helmet to head a ball, especially if it had been raining, when its weight was doubled. Boots were over the ankle with large studs 'which hurt when you ran over another player's back'. The football shirts were generally one size, which was fine if you were that size but hard lines if you were not. As Charlie observed,

"They wear their names on their shirts now, when we played you were lucky if you got a number, and even luckier if it fitted."

It wasn't as bad as the joke might imply but it is impossible to draw any similarities between that era and the current day. There were few really big salary earners in those days with the Fulham and England inside forward Johnnie Haynes being the first footballer to command one hundred pounds per week. Charlie never aspired to those heights but he enjoyed a reasonably well-paid career, although he never earned enough to guarantee a secure future and so a job would be vital when his career finally ended.

But Charlie does not resent the high earners of today's football, even if he does feel that the money they earn is 'immoral'.

He was never one to outstay his invitation and so early in 1963 he finally contemplated retirement. His love of the game never left him, so that non-league football beckoned and with it a guaranteed weekly fee to keep the wolf from the door.

It was at that time that George Rayner moved on, leaving the job of manager up for grabs resulting in a number of applicants and Charlie decided to throw his hat into the ring. He was pleased to be placed on the short list, but was in direct competition with Jimmy Maddison who was subsequently offered the job. The *Skegness Standard* covered the outcome of the Club's deliberations in a report on the 15th August 1962,

"Former club skipper, Charlie Williams has rejected Town's offer for the following season. He was until a few weeks ago on the short list as player-manager. He is saying goodbye to the Town and may be quitting soccer. This is a surprise move and has shocked local supporters and members of the committee also.

"Charlie has rejected the terms offered to him and stated that he would be moving back to his native Yorkshire.

"For Charlie, the cheerful centre-half who joined Town from second division Doncaster Rovers in 1959 and became captain almost immediately he started, the last three months have been a time of doubt and indecision.

"In May a committee meeting attended by only eleven of the fifteen members decided not to retain him. The decision is believed to have been a split vote and at a later meeting the four absent committee members including Chairman Councillor Harold Swift, managed not only to reverse the decision but also offer Williams the post of Player-Manager. He said he would like the job and would be considered for the post along with another candidate Jimmy Maddison. However, on another close decision the club chose Maddison.

Charlie was then offered terms as a player but at a much lower wage than the previous season. He refused to sign, "I have served the club as well as the next man and know of two more players who are getting much more than me. It is a matter of principle."

Chairman Harold Swift tried to persuade the committee to raise the offer on more than one occasion, but without success and Charlie refused once again to accept the original terms offered.

In May 1962 Charlie lost both jobs in the same week. He was sacked by the Football Club and the firm he was working for (Haywoods Rock Factory) closed down.

Charlie set up a window-cleaning business in partnership with Town trainer Jimmy Walker, but the round was not big enough in the winter to give both men a decent living wage."

Charlie had his dignity and it would not be for the last time that his self-respect forbade him to loose faith in himself.   He turned down the offer of a smaller contract and left Skegness.   Once again he had reached a turning point in his life as he looked elsewhere for a job.

Denaby Main Football Club made him an offer and Charlie accepted it; it was time to move on to pastures new.   Denaby is a village near Doncaster where the men are men and so are some of the women.   They take their football very seriously and play with a passion as though their lives depended on it and it has been said of some of the endogenous population that they would rather 'fight than have a hot dinner'.   Charlie did not accept that proposition, saying that the Denaby people were some of the best he had ever met but there was no doubt the football team contained some 'hard men'.

"There were no poofs in that side," said Charlie.

Denaby Main F.C. provided a continuation to his football career and an enjoyable Saturday run-out, and the camaraderie was good, but without a full-time occupation Charlie had difficulties making ends meet.   He had been used to a regular income but then suddenly it stopped. The dole queue was staring him full in the face.

Chapter Eight

THE AUSTRALIAN INCIDENT

Once again his old friend Alick Jeffrey was to play a part in the next phase of his career. He had kept in touch with Charlie reporting upon the beautiful country, the year-round sunshine and of course a lucrative contract which included a house and car. Alick was playing regularly and was achieving a great deal of success, so much so that his credibility with the management of the team had allowed him a powerful voice in an advisory capacity within the club as well as on the pitch. When he heard of Charlie's pending retirement he recommended him to the manager to work as player-coach. Charlie took only a short time to consider the offer. It was a lifeline and with a two year contract against nothing else in the pipeline it's not difficult to see why he accepted it.

All the arrangements were made and Charlie had even agreed the leasing of his house for the two year period of the contract. He could not believe how easy it was, but just prior to departure date Charlie sent his passport to Australia House. The acknowledgement he received was not what he expected.

The local press had carried features about Charlie's career from its inception and the 'Australian incident' was to invoke more publicity than anyone could have imagined. Headlines such as 'Charlie goes down under' and 'New lease of life for local football star' carried the story for days prior to the bombshell which burst around his ears when the reply from Australia House landed on his breakfast table. It seems that Charlie had qualified in just about every particular except for his colour. When the passport had revealed that Charlie was black, the offer of the contract, the car and the house in the sun were withdrawn.

Inevitably the press became involved and for once the crusade was in support and the destructive abilities of the newspapers were turned on the Australians highlighting the spectre of racial prejudice.

The *Barnsley Chronicle* started it all and when they got as far as they could the national press took over. The Australian embassy was harangued by every paper taking up the gauntlet. Charlie became the subject of a national incident and whilst headlines were being made, the pressure upon Australia House intensified.

Eventually the Australian press became involved and what started as a simple rebuke against a coloured sportsman ended up with the potential to damage the very fabric of the Australian government. The Prime Minister of the time, Robert Menzies, realised the dangerous potential of what had happened and the result was a carefully worded statement pointing out that there was no colour bar in Australia. Shortly afterwards the offer was renewed and the press were elated but Charlie turned the offer down. It was not just a knee-jerk reaction brought about by a man scorned, but more of an inclination to follow his heart.

He considered that the offer was being made under sufferance and as such he would have been working at a considerable disadvantage. It was not an appropriate platform from which to work and although he admits he may have been cynical at the time, subsequent events have proved him right. He never shirked from a challenge, but in that case the odds were far from fair. He admits now to a feeling of disappointment and even annoyance at the way he was treated, but accepts that fate had the final say and pointed him in the direction of the labour exchange.

It was quite ironic that in 1975 the then disablement resettlement officer, Bill Harman, booked Charlie as the guest celebrity to open the Barnsley Job Centre.

Chapter Nine

DOLE QUEUE

In the initial stages Charlie avoided the dole queue as a matter of dignity and for a time he lived off his savings, but when they had been depleted, he had no option but to join the ranks of the unemployed. It was the thing that caused him the most fear. Some people worry about health, children, divorced parents and so on, but Charlie's nightmare was being unemployed. He accepts that his pride was at the root of this concern, but he was entitled to that, and those weeks of queuing in the labour exchange as it was then, were the worst of his life. There are those who make a vocation of their joustings with the unemployment officer, but not Charlie. He genuinely wished to work and hated being denied self-sufficiency as well as the humiliation which he felt at being without a job.

He began his search for a job but unfortunately his reputation as a footballer did not help him as employers had little interest in his past. He concedes that if he had been a latter day George Best or Bobby Moore then he would have been able to bring his prestige to the interviewer's table, but the reality was that he had been a second division footballer who played the game and did very well, but in those days it did not carry with it the glories of today. His career was ended and the cold, hard reality of being one of many with an illustrious past counted for nothing but a nod and a pat on the back, and perhaps a free drink if he had chosen to haunt the supporters' clubs

He attended a number of interviews, but he had no training or particular skill other than in football. He had been a driver whilst at Skegness, but such jobs were few and far between and there was no mint rock with the word *Barnsley* printed through it. One day however, he secured an interview with a baking firm who used a number of roundsmen to deliver bread and confectionery direct to their customers' doors in company vans specially adapted for the purpose.

Charlie attended the interview and recalled the occasion very well,

"You're a smart lad," said the baker. "You're clean and tidy and well presented and there's no doubt you could do the job, but you do have one small problem." It was an attempt by an otherwise ignorant man to deal with a very difficult situation. He failed miserably and told Charlie what someone with a little tact would have couched in different terms.

"You can understand it can't you," he said, "but our customers might be funny about a coloured bloke delivering bread. It might put them off and I can't afford to lose trade."

It was the matter of fact way in which the body-blow had been delivered which hurt him most. Perhaps it was asking a lot to expect a 'bit of tact', but Charlie was not in a position to argue and years of self-discipline taught him to turn the other cheek. This time the newspapers did not fly to his aid.

Charlie was unemployed for nearly nine months, a period which he describes as being one of the worst times of his life as the weekly visits to the dole queue and the labour exchange whittled away at his dignity like rats at a grain-sack.

During this period he completed his contract with Denaby but then he was invited to play for the Grimethorpe Colliery football team in one of the northern leagues. He was to be paid three pounds a match and so things began to look up.

The never-ending list of interviews grew longer as the months passed by, until Charlie was given the opportunity of a meeting with a local scrap dealer. It was a meeting and not an interview. The prospective employer was Ernie Sykes, a local minor-league entrepreneur who cared little for racial problems, being too busy making money to consider conflict. He needed a driver-labourer. It was a hard, dirty job, and one where most of Charlie's potential work-mates ended up being the same colour as himself at the end of the working day.

"The only trouble was when we all showered they went back to being white and I stayed as I was!"

Charlie learned the tricks of the scrap trade from his boss who was a likeable rogue, but one who would - "Gladly cut a currant in two rather than use a full 'un!"

He was paid the princely sum of ten pounds per week, but it was hard and dirty work. His job involved the carriage of scrap from place to place and he was taught to check all the containers when he collected his load to ensure they had not been filled with water. It was an old dodge used to increase the weight and therefore the price. He would then drive the lorry to its destination for a 'back to back sale', pausing en route only to fill up any containers with water so as to increase the weight.

It was a whole new way of life for Charlie and in many ways it was a retrograde step almost back to his days as a miner.   He did not enjoy his days 'in scrap' but in the absence of any alternative, it was a job with a small but regular income.   Fortunately and fatefully Charlie had maintained his interest in the entertainment scene.   He entered talent competitions in the pubs and clubs leading to a booking every so often for a few pounds, which helped out when the wages ran out, but he had not quite mastered the act which was to make him famous.   He was a singer with a pleasant voice, but his aspirations only extended to weekend bookings and a reasonable reception for his songs.   In fact he received more than a reasonable reception and with it a degree of popularity which was to lead to regular bookings.

He declined all offers of management agencies who wished to claim his services.   Charlie was not one for signing contracts either, preferring to give his word as his bond, with a verbal agreement confirmed by a handshake. He was never to break any such agreement.

Over the years, Charlie changed and improved his act but as his repertoire of songs diminished, the comedy element of the act increased to a point where Charlie grew into being a stand-up comedian.   His act was simple, a series of well-timed jokes poignantly aimed at everyday life, in a language that everyone could understand and with a marked absence of filth.

He was aided of course by his intrinsic gift of timing, which amounted to over fifty per cent of the quality of story-telling.   His material was interesting because he did not use a series of gag-writers, but his jokes were based upon his life experiences and a keen sense of observation. He also had an excellent memory which served him well, adding to his repertoire of jokes and stories saved from his time in the mines.

A fascinating thing about comedians is that they attract the attentions of would-be comics who want to tell them the latest jokes, and Charlie took advantage of their generosity to build up a considerable repertoire without the luxury but attendant expense of gag writers.

Charlie had fond memories of those early days in the clubs, where the larger the club and the bigger the turn-over, the more professional the equipment. The piano gave way to the electric organ and voices were aided by amplification and the start of sophisticated technology and 'reverb'.

There were days Charlie recalls, where the audiences were exceptionally polite and artists, particularly good ones, were assured of every courtesy. It was however, the beginnings of the era of the pop group and the electronic guitar and in clubland, as in the mining communities, times were changing, but not all for the better.

Charlie was never one to be idle and he was offered a place in the Grimethorpe Colliery football team at three pounds a match. His standard had lost some of its sparkle but he still excelled at that level. The result was he helped the team gain promotion to a higher league in his first season. He was still pursuing his clubland career and with perseverance and an iron determination the bookings increased. He adopted the stage name of Mel Williams and began to enjoy considerable success, perceiving a welcome and discernible light at the end of the tunnel with a regular income from a job and the odd pound or two from his footballing. Charlie began to think that the loss of the job in Australia was probably not such a bad thing after all.

On his travels he came in touch with the then ubiquitous workingmen's club concert secretary, a strange hybrid who had sprung up in the fifties and sixties to channel a positive new area of entertainment seekers in a setting akin to that of the local pub. In some ways it was a throw-back to the music halls of Charlie's youth, but it's popularity had begun to gain considerable momentum and with it came the club agent.

Chapter Ten

THE WORKINGMEN'S CLUBS

In the early 1960's the workingmen's club had formulated the idea of the 'showcase' which brought a number of acts into the spotlight to show their skills and hopefully encourage bookings. There was competition between clubs as to who could provide the best evenings out, but of course the clubs had budgets and the financial constraints imposed by the committees had to be observed. The workingmen's club was a peculiarly autonomous body; run by the committee on behalf of it's members. The committees were comprised of ardent club-goers and people who liked to be on committees.

The showcase was also a useful vehicle for the local agents to see acts old and new as they performed free of charge, in the hope of attracting work. If an aspiring artiste performed well at one of these functions, he or she might secure a number of bookings, or even better an agent to obtain work for them. Theatres had begun to lose their popularity and were systematically taken over by bingo clubs so that the workingmen's clubs became the only showcase for live entertainment.

Generally speaking, the relationship between the agent and the club was a reasonable one: on the one hand the agent needed the clubs to provide work for his artistes and the clubs needed the agent to vet and provide suitable acts for their members. There were good acts, average acts and not so good acts, but then there were good clubs, not so good clubs and 'the lions' den'. The ingredient for a successful club act was talent, a good amplifier and a thick skin.

Charlie attended the showcase venues and was beginning to formulate a solo act since Alick Jeffrey was in Australia and Alick's father had retired leaving Charlie free to 'paddle his own canoe'. He had begun to build on his singing act and comic introductions to his songs by telling the odd joke or two, because he had seen the amused reaction to his broad South Yorkshire accent and local sayings, mingled with references to his colour and his forebears. The more he introduced racist humour turned against himself, the more accepted he became and the more popular he found himself to be with a growing list of clubs who were re-booking him.

He told jokes and stories against himself to find that he was becoming known as one of the most original acts in clubland and the more jokes he told, the better the audience reacted to him.

Charlie was never one to miss an opportunity and neither were a number of concert secretaries at the time, since they too had seen the potential of this comedian with his quips about tin baths and Nigerian lager. It was material, of course, which no-one else could use and so Charlie began to evolve a most unique style. There was no doubt that there was something quite novel about a black man telling jokes in a broad South Yorkshire accent, with material which was never blue but rich in tales of everyday life, to audiences who could identify with him. His act was a paradox, a contradiction in terms.

Weekends were the most productive times because the 'noon and nighter' proved popular and took the form of a double booking on Sundays, with performances at Sunday lunch-time and also in the evening. Inevitably he had the same audience on Sunday lunch-time as on Sunday nights and so the material as well as the songs had to be different. This meant an extension of his act, but Charlie was realising how popular his material was: the more jokes he told, the more popular he became.

Charlie recalled one incident in a workingmen's club in Doncaster when a concert secretary spoke to him after his act to say how much he had enjoyed Charlie's jokes; but made no mention of any of the songs. Charlie could take a hint and with that he became a comic.

Unfortunately there were no classes or tuition available for the aspiring comedian. Guitarists could take lessons, as could singers, but there were no comedy tutors. It was purely and simply a question of talent and experience, so he listened and memorised the jokes of the day, adding them to his act when he thought they were good enough. It was true that competition was fierce, but Charlie had a great advantage in being the only black comedian around, and as such there could be little or no challenge from others, with the end result that all the local clubs got to know about the black comedian from Barnsley.

As the clubs prospered, so did the agents and so did the acts whom they were called upon to represent. Charlie was as popular as any other act and return bookings were the 'norm'. His diary was filling up and occasionally he was faced with performing at two clubs in one night, so that it was not unusual for him to be booked for an early evening performance in Doncaster and a late spot in Barnsley. Sometimes the same acts would be on the bill and he would cross with them as they were travelling to their respective clubs.

Working between two clubs was always difficult and whilst it provided a change of venue, it afforded a stressful degree of travelling with the constant worry that you would not arrive on time. Charlie suffered the stress because he was a stickler for good time-keeping, a legacy from his time in the pit, for late-comers missed the cage and consequently a shift.

The hardest job of all was doing three spots in one club, during which they would sometimes be expected to perform for thirty to forty-five minutes per spot, which required a great deal of material, and it was on these occasions that Charlie's singing voice came in handy to add a little variety.

There are many stories in clubland concerning artistes who drank so much that their performance suffered and there were also the acts who were not well prepared, but Charlie had his feet firmly on the floor and his eyes focused on the performance. He neither drank before a show nor indeed during it. He was almost manic about time-keeping and in between his spots he kept himself to himself, preferring to concentrate on the next part of his act than to consume copious amounts of free drinks from admirers. Needless to say his professionalism helped his popularity, for reliability was almost as important as the quality of the performance.

Charlie was charm itself, and with his inbuilt ability to be able to get on with everybody, he managed to get through his first year in clubland without making enemies; a feat of considerable proportions in itself.

He performed in all manner of establishments from pubs to church halls and community centres to workingmen's clubs. There were venues with sound equipment and venues without, good audiences and rowdy ones, but in the main he was well received. He experimented with his performance, changing jokes and the general pattern of his material, blending humour with vocals and playing to the audience's proclivity to associate with their past. He told jokes about bath-night and haemorrhoids and all the time the audience empathised with him. They knew exactly what he meant. He told it as it was, highlighting facets of everyday life which everyone could understand. One observer was overheard to pay a truly backhanded compliment which was probably inverted racism when he turned to a friend after Charlie had finished his act and said,

"It's not as if he's black, he's nearly one of us."

Charlie has since observed,

"Well I'm halfway there at least."

The question remains as to which half and where.

It was not all a bed of roses and there were times when Charlie thought he could have done much better things with his time, but the bookings kept coming in with reasonable fees, which managed to keep the wolf from the door and his insecurity at bay.

Whatever the criticisms of northern clubland, it was a training ground for artistes of all descriptions who had nowhere else to learn the profession. Theatres continued to close, leaving clubs to reign supreme so far as live entertainment was concerned and the maxim 'you either work clubs or you don't work' was never more apparent than in that era.

The concert secretary was an interesting character and in many of the clubs in the north he was usually retired, wore a flat cap, smoked a pipe or Woodbines, spoke with a heavy pronounced Yorkshire accent, had a limp and a glass eye, and claimed to know everything about the noble profession of show-business. It would not be fair to generalise, but basically this was the character who dictated to the acts of the day. His character was beautifully depicted in the stage act of Norman Collier when he donned his flat cap, limped across the stage and feigned the perils of a faulty microphone, providing the most hilarious innuendo to what the audience knew he intended to say.

Another expert in the parody of the concert secretary was the late Colin Crompton who started his television career in *The Comedians*. He also appeared regularly with fellow comedian Bernard Manning in a spin-off programme from *The Comedians* called The Wheeltappers and Shunters Social Club. Crompton played the part of the concert secretary: with cigarette in hand and flat cap on head he perpetually rang the house bell to bring the audience to order and announced such worth-while snippets as,

"The steward says the pies have come," and

"'Arry says the gents' toilet is unblocked and he's now ready to serve the pies."

There were two prime factions to overcome in the clubs: on the one hand you had to satisfy the audience, but more importantly you had to gain acceptance from the concert secretary. If you satisfied both, you were a success. If you failed, you were not re-booked. Charlie was lucky because he qualified on both counts, enjoying a great rapport with the concert secretaries, even the one with the flat cap, the glass eye and the limp!

Charlie was performing in one Barnsley club when the concert secretary, (who is now deceased), pointed out that the song was in a key which was too high and he could not join in. It was a rather inopportune remark for him to have made, particularly as Charlie was in mid-song, but he dealt with the incident most diplomatically and thanked the secretary for the benefit of his greater knowledge. He turned to the organist and drummer and shouted,

"A much lower key please."

In a whisper he told the organist that he couldn't sing it in a much lower key, so the musicians carried on exactly as before. During the song Charlie glanced at the concert secretary for approval, who gave him the thumbs up sign and mouthed the words, "That's better," as he continued to smoke his pipe, read the *'Clubman's Guide'* and sing completely out of tune.

There was a great deal of camaraderie amongst the artistes and Charlie's popularity with others of his kind is well exemplified in Duggie Brown's tribute when describing him as 'one of the lads', with a reputation for gentlemanly behaviour, his word being his bond. The entertainer and radio personality Tony Capstick remembered Charlie for his kindness and consideration.

"Charlie was my hero. He had got that lovely way with him that endeared him to an audience. He could tackle even the hardest of clubs and find an affinity with the most difficult of audiences. He could go where many of us feared to tread."

All Charlie needed was the one big break. Fortuitously, the opportunity did not arrive until Charlie was good and ready, and when it did, he took full advantage of a ball delivered to his feet.

He was quite happy with the way his career was going since he was working regularly and his entertaining abilities brought luxuries which other families could not afford. His family were always at the forefront of his spending, but Charlie was not extravagant and his past had taught him to be thrifty.

Chapter Eleven

SEMI-PROFESSIONAL COMEDIAN

Up to 1970 Charlie organised his own bookings, without an agent or manager and it wasn't until Stanley Joseph arrived on the scene that he used an agent at all. Charlie was motivated by his desire for security rather than greed and whereas many acts would try to squeeze every penny out of their paymasters, Charlie agreed to accept what he thought was fair and left it at that. There was no whinging and whining from him.

"I was never a greedy person, and I always had my eye on the future. If the audience liked me and the club respected me in my dealings, they would always ask me back. I have seen many an act blacked (if you'll pardon the expression!) by excessive demands and unprofessional behaviour. I always liked to attend a booking ten minutes before I was due to be there. I suppose it started when I was in the pits, when you had to be there on time to catch the transport down to the coal face. I always found that if you were late for a function, it immediately put you under pressure and allowed your mind to waver from your act. Comedy is a very serious business and your mind has to be focused and you have to concentrate fully on the task ahead. I was never one for playing practical jokes or having a good drink before a performance. I liked to sit quietly and reflect before I went on. I like to think that I was very professional."

A workingmen's club can be a fountain of camaraderie and fun but some clubs are inhabited by people who want to talk and even shout over the music and compete with the comedians. Quite why these people turn up at all defies understanding and these sort of clubs did little for the cause of clubland, except to establish a reputation which was not truly representative of them all. Artistes kept blacklists of the clubs to avoid but some just took the money and put up with it.

There were clubs where the maxim was 'the customers are always right', but at one club a note on the wall in the artistes dressing-room proclaimed 'the customers are always shite'.

Charlie was due to appear in Middlesborough, long believed to be one of the comedians' graveyards. An appearance at this particular club was more like an initiation ceremony into a violent cult than an exploitation of South Yorkshire humour.

It was an old-fashioned club where half-pint glasses did not exist unless they were used to hold brandy and Babycham. Beer was the biggest seller followed by mild and then whisky. No-one had heard of gin and tonic and tequila sunrise had to wait some years to reach the menu. There was sawdust on the floor and standing at the bar was reserved for only the most accurate in the face of the spittoons. The concert room was a male preserve, where the women knew their place and no-one drank from a bottle. The era of the glassless drinker was still far off into the future.

It was 8pm and Charlie was about to perform his first spot. His introduction from the Concert Secretary could be best described as basic.

"Here is your turn for tonight - he calls himself a comedian and you know how we like comedians - here is Charlie Williams!"
The reaction to his entrance was as if he had set foot into a Ku Klux Klan meeting in the deep south of America.

"Good evening, my flowers."
The audience looked as if in a state of shock and the only way to cope with the condition was to remain silent. It was as if the audience had seen their first Martian.
Charlie opened with a song and when he hit the last note they were still open-mouthed until his first joke made one of the inmates on the front row smile. The second brought a chuckle and the third had them laughing. By the end of the first spot Charlie had become their favourite comedian.

"Tha's done well," said the concert secretary, "You'll get out in one piece now."

"Is that a compliment?" asked Charlie.

"Arghh," said the concert secretary. "By the way, you can come back on Boxing Day - oh and how did you manage to get that accent, you do ever so well. I should keep it, you've got a good idea there."
The concert secretary was right for once, and Charlie returned on Boxing Day when he was the only comedian white or black to re-appear at that club in the same year.
When Charlie returned home, he told one of his clubland friends where he had been. The latter marvelled at Charlie's injury-free face and realised that having got out of that club unscathed, he must surely be destined for stardom.
It was one of many clubs to fall under his spell; the north of England liked him and understood him. He spoke of

everyday life in such a way as to make the audience identify with him and his natural charm won over even the most hostile of audiences.   He became the talk of Clubland and the clubs themselves were beginning to realise the extent of Charlie's popularity in the most persuasive of terms - whenever he appeared on the bill, the club was full and beer sales doubled.

Charlie was happy with his new-found success but in certain clubs he was subject to 'Concert Secretary's Commission' whereby a £15 booking meant £13 for him and £2 for the concert secretary.   The widespread use of 'back-handing' was finding its way into the concert room and Charlie found that at certain clubs you either joined in or you didn't work.

Despite his rather localised success, Charlie had not given much thought to his long-term future.   It was not a question of a singular lack of ambition, but more a case of treating his life on a week by week basis, taking everything as it came as a new experience, not daring to plan for fear it might go as quickly as it came.

On the one hand, he was open and rather gregarious in his performance but when he had finished the act he reverted to his rather quiet self to snatch such time for privacy as his dual employment would allow.   He made many friends in show-biz and although his time was dedicated to work as opposed to socialising, he was nevertheless very popular as the Yorkshire comedian Duggie Brown recalls,

"When I am out, the first person I am asked about is Charlie."

Eric Todd was a show-business writer for a number of the local papers who spent a substantial period of his time travelling the clubs and reporting upon acts from far and wide. He has some special memories of Charlie Williams.

"I have been a journalist in showbusiness for over thirty years and during that time I have seen and reported on a substantial number of artistes.

"Charlie first came to my attention when he was in the Alick Jeffrey Duo and thereafter as a solo singer and then comedian. I was one of the organisers of the Clubland Awards Show which Charlie won in 1970. After that he never looked back.

"I remember him coming to my house the day before the big show, when it became apparent to me that he did not have any publicity photographs or advertising material. I remember that we had to sit and take some photographs in my front room so that we could create a portfolio. Needless to say, he won the competition and the rest, as they say, is history."

Chapter Twelve

TURNING PRO

T he Yorkshire club scene was at the height of its popularity with artistes performing almost every night of the week, in hundreds of clubs. Charlie's own popularity had increased enormously between the years of 1965 and 1970, so much so, that he found himself performing nearly every night of the week, in addition to holding down a full-time job and playing football on Saturdays. The problem was that he was being asked to perform further afield, which inevitably meant an increase in travelling to and from the respective venues. Charlie had built up a reputation and a clientele amongst so many clubs that he was able to pick and choose where he wanted to perform. He recalls those heady days with much affection, particularly from the point of view of the audiences who were always appreciative and so friendly.

As the 1970s approached, Charlie was facing some important decisions. It was no longer possible to continue his full-time job and his act, but Charlie had known adversity and the old problem of insecurity was never far away. Once again, fate was to take a hand and this time introduced Charlie to Stanley and Michael Joseph, the famous theatrical agents who were to play a decisive role in his career. The Joseph brothers own and run ATS Casting of Leeds, a most famous and prestigious show-business agency. Their father owned the Lewisham Hippodrome, bought a theatre in Blackpool in

1939 and also acquired the lease for the world-famous City Varieties Theatre in Leeds. During and after the war years, he concentrated on the development of the theatre, turning it into a household name.

His two sons, Stanley and Michael were indoctrinated into show life and when their father died they took over the business, calling upon their considerable experience of all matters theatrical.

The brothers remember meeting Charlie for the first time, when he and they paid a special visit to the Ace Club in Wakefield, a regular meeting place for many of the local artistes and members of the theatrical profession. The brothers had seen Charlie before and had watched and studied his act. They were impressed with Charlie's style, so reminiscent of the great music hall comedians of the past, and after a short time, discussions were opened between them which were to form the basis of a long and profitable relationship for both sides.

The Joseph brothers were very influential agents indeed, with a large number of top-billing acts on their books. Many artistes would have given anything to be represented by them, and like most agents they were inundated with calls from aspiring singers, dancers, comedians and actors, all seeking support in their quest for fame and fortune. The approach was usually made by the artiste, but in Charlie's case it was the other way round.

Michael Joseph had no doubt that Charlie was a highly marketable commodity, being able to adapt his material for theatre and a family audience, as well as satisfying the cabaret and night-club scene. The agreement was made with a handshake and during the 25 years they represented him, there was never a written contract. Stanley Joseph saw no point and indeed still adopts the same principle: that if an artiste is unhappy there is no point holding him to an agreement. It simply does not work and on the basis that the Joseph brothers are still here and are still doing the business, who is to say that they were wrong?

It was a happy liaison, with Charlie ever the hard worker, desperate to succeed and prove his point. He hated being idle and was never happier than when his diary was full. Stanley recalled,

"He had all the discipline of one of the great comics, but he had a feeling for the audience and they for him, and it was in live entertainment that he really shone. In Charlie's case he played the role of Charlie Williams playing himself and at that he had no equal."

The agency still operates from premises in Leeds and their large office contains a number of filing cabinets neatly set out and arranged within the office. In the fourth filing cabinet there was a file marked 'Charlie Williams' remarkably devoid of correspondence. When I queried the extent of the file I was told that 'the better the artiste, the thinner the file'. It transpired that Charlie was a true professional and did not cause problems for the agency by excessive or frivolous demands, consequently there was no necessity to engage in long and protracted correspondence. The majority of the contact was by telephone and Charlie was given a list of dates and he dutifully obliged.

"It was inevitable," said Stanley Joseph, "that if Charlie was to further his career, he had to take the giant step into turning professional. I never thought for a minute that he would be anything less than successful. Within a relatively short time of us acting on his behalf, Charlie took that step. There was no doubt in my mind that he was going to be a great success."

It is unlikely that Charlie realised at the time that he was heading for star status. He really didn't consider the proposition as he spent the majority of his time listening, learning and perfecting his art, but once again insecurity proved to be the spur and with persistence, hard work and a great amount of talent, Charlie was on his way. He had previously left the scrap-yard and had taken a job in the equipment repair room back with the NCB at Shafton. It was a wrench to give up this sheet-anchor but it was inevitable.

At first he integrated his own bookings into those which the Joseph brothers arranged for him but he insisted on honouring every existing contract, even if he could have earned more by reneging on bookings and taking better ones elsewhere.

The Agency's influence did not just extend to clubland, but also into cabaret, night-clubs and the theatres which were still popular and attracting good sized audiences. Whilst Charlie was the king of the club scene, Stanley Joseph's quest was to introduce him to a wider audience on a national basis. Like so many other talented artistes, Charlie needed a bit of luck but he would not have long to wait. It was to arrive in the form of the television producer Johnnie Hamp.

Chapter Thirteen

THE COMEDIANS

Johnny Hamp was the controller of light entertainment at Granada Television in the early seventies and he is an acknowledged expert in such matters. One of the benefits of his job was to visit theatres and clubs and watch entertainers to obtain ideas for future programmes.

Johnnie found that the comedian in a show was rarely, if ever, the top billing artiste and yet so far as the audience was concerned he was an integral, if not the most important, member of the cast, providing the balance needed for variety.

The usual equation in variety was a singer, a speciality act, dancers and a comedian, but Johnnie was looking for a new idea, something different that would appeal to a large audience.

A show consisting entirely of singers would be unlikely to attract the media attention required for this sort of idea and it was unlikely that audiences would enjoy a stream of magicians or people making dachshunds out of balloons, but a show comprising comedians only, would be another thing altogether.

It was a brilliant innovation, but the cost of staging such a venture with the top comedians of the day would have been prohibitive. It was against this background that Johnnie Hamp decided to trawl the northern clubs and select a cast from the pick of the comedians doing the rounds on the local circuit.

He started in Manchester and realised just how many excellent comedians there were. His journeys also took him to the home of clubland in Yorkshire which provided a rich seam of comedians and Johnnie spent a great deal of time visiting clubs and watching the acts perform. He kept lists of the comedians who made him laugh and many of them came from Yorkshire.

Fate had decreed that Johnnie should visit a club in the Leeds area, where he had heard of a black comedian with a marked Yorkshire accent called Charlie Williams and such an act would add that difference or perhaps a further dimension to a programme consisting entirely of comedians.

Johnnie recalls that performance,

"Apart from his excellent timing, his broad Yorkshire accent combined with his black face really caught the imagination of the audience."

He added Charlie's name to the shortlist, but accepts that his decision was made that day and once again the selling points were Charlie's colour and his God-given talent to make people laugh. In a simple phrase, "He was unique" and once again his colour provided the advantage. Johnnie approached Charlie that night and mentioned the series to him, when a meeting was arranged to discuss the details. For Charlie, it was a rendezvous with destiny.

After a long period of research Johnnie drew up a final list of participants. The first series included the following:

> Duggie Brown
> Frank Carson
> Mike Coyne
> Ken Goodwin

Bernard Manning
Paul Melba
George Roper and Charlie

Charlie knew many of the cast from his travels on the club circuit and the first rehearsal was a laugh a minute, so much so that the only problem was knowing what to cut out. The banter between the comics provided much hilarity not only for them, but also the technicians and the administrative staff who were involved in the show.

There was a real buzz of excitement in the studio and it was apparent to everyone that Johnnie had something very special on his hands. Nevertheless he was able to construct the programme quite cheaply and the comedians were delighted to get the opportunity of exposure to the wider audiences which television would bring. It was the 'potential' factor which was Johnnie's main weapon in his dealings with the comedians and their agents.

Stanley and Michael Joseph were delighted that Charlie had been given the opportunity to trade his wares before a live television audience and they knew that Charlie would shine in those circumstances, in what could only be a golden opportunity. If it worked, his value would increase substantially and with it the amount of his fees.

Charlie did not quite realise the true potential of this quantum leap. He thought and realised that the words 'as seen on T.V.' were as valuable in entertaining parlance as 'by Royal appointment' but he had not realised that the show would catapult him to national fame.

Johnnie did his best to recreate the atmosphere which prevailed in the theatres and clubs, choosing to place his performers before a live studio audience.

It worked. The first show went out and the audience in the studio loved it and so did the critics. The television pages of the newspapers waxed lyrical about the new innovative programme simply entitled *The Comedians*. One artiste stood out more than the rest; a black comedian with a broad south Yorkshire accent called Charlie Williams. The audience loved him. To use a Yorkshire expression, he had 'cracked it' and the opportunities which this success afforded him were endless. Charlie seized the chance with both hands. He was to become a national star, although he took it all in his stride.

Life in show-business is hard.   The most talented of people rarely make the big time and the theatres and clubs are littered with performers of great ability, but then so is the dole queue.   The difficulty is being 'discovered'.   The big organisations with their main agents, record companies and the like determine who gets a chance and who does not, but of course fate plays more than a supporting role, so that talent is not always a deciding factor.

If an artiste is really lucky and gets into the big time, all sorts of pressures impinge on the recipient's future path. Lesser mortals cannot cope with stardom, some become insufferable, but some take it all in their stride.   One such person was Charlie Williams.

Stanley and Michael Joseph capitalised on Charlie's new-found success and were able to negotiate excellent fees and a better class of venue.   If there was a downside it was the enormous amount of travelling which plundered his free time, and his suitcase and tuxedo became his constant companions.

Prior to *The Comedians*, the majority of Charlie's bookings were within his own locality and he managed to have time at home during the day, but following his success he had no option but to work farther afield.

His family were to see less and less of him and with his success came the inevitable regret. Success had its price.

Chapter Fourteen

THE LONDON PALLADIUM
AND OTHER THEATRES

By 1972, *The Comedians* television programme had reached a high point in its popularity and the Saturday early evening performance achieved fantastic viewing figures. It was a smash hit, but there was more in store.

Johnnie Hamp had formed two separate teams of comedians to keep the programme fresh. In one team there was Charlie, the Lancastrian Ken Goodwin, southerner Dave Butler, sadly now deceased, the Londoner Mike Reid, the Liverpudlian Jos White (the only other coloured comedian in the set-up) and the Mancunian Bernard Manning.

The other team comprised of the Irishman Frank Carson, the Yorkshireman Duggie Brown, the Lancastrian Colin Compton, the Mancunian George Roper and the Londoner Mike Burton.

During the passage of time other comedians joined their ranks. Johnnie Hamp had been discussing his project with a number of agents and theatrical managers and he decided to take the show on tour. Bernard Delfont came to Leeds, watched a performance, liked what he saw and offered *The Comedians* a short season at the London Palladium. He felt that the whole idea was innovative and with the eye of the seasoned professional, the gamble was taken. Charlie found Bernard Delfont to be an extremely good businessman, with a good eye and nose for success. He was not known to enjoy failures and the fact that he had backed *The Comedians* show and offered them the Palladium just added even more to their kudos. Charlie and his team were engaged to 'test the water.' The show was a huge and immediate success and played to sell-out audiences every night.   There were thirteen shows a week, with Sunday the only day off. The 'short run' which was envisaged to take but a few weeks extended into six months.   It was a very lucrative engagement, but inevitably there was a price to pay as Charlie was only to see his family on Sunday mornings, because the evenings were taken up with a series of special summer concerts in coastal areas.

Initially, the comedians lived in small hotels until they realised that their contract was to be extended and consequently Charlie decided to minimise his costs and rent a small flat.   His choice of flat-mate was the black comedian Jos White.   They were good friends and had an easygoing relationship, and on the basis that they would be working and living together, it was essential that they should get on.   Charlie describes the relationship as 'the odd couple' for on the one hand he was meticulously tidy and organised and on the other Jos was simply 'the untidiest bugger alive'.   Jos did have one major talent however which was in the art of nouvelle cuisine, for he was a superb chef.   Allowances therefore had to be made, so Charlie took on the duties of maid, whilst Jos became head cook and bottle-washer. The arrangement worked extremely well, although neither of them thought that they would be working in London for up to six months.   Charlie was not in awe of his revered surroundings and to him the Palladium was just another theatre, but it was a very good career move and one which was to steadfastly protect and secure his finances for the foreseeable future.

Charlie did not know how long his success was to last, although *The Comedians* had brought him national fame, and so he decided to work as hard as he could whilst he could.

If there was a problem with the show at the Palladium it was the uncertainty as to how long the season would last. All the comedians had other bookings and commitments and systematically they had to be cancelled as the season continued. Bernard Delfont was never one to ruin a good thing and whilst the money came in at the box office, the show continued its run.

Whilst Charlie enjoyed the shows and the camaraderie with the other comedians, he was becoming increasingly aware that his family were seeing little or nothing of him. It was not practical to move his family to London, for his children were too young. There was a house to upkeep and the flat was barely large enough for Charlie and Jos without having a woman and two small children in occupation as well. The other point was that the cast worked on a fortnightly basis, never really knowing when it would end.

The success of the Palladium show prompted Bernard Delfont to book *The Comedians* for the Royal Variety Command Performance and there could be no doubt that this was the supreme accolade. In those days the Command Performance attracted massive viewing figures on television and was well-known for making the careers of many artistes who were introduced to a national audience. It was the icing on the cake for Charlie, because he had had massive television coverage with *The Comedians* and then to find himself on the biggest variety show in the country ensured his place in the popularity stakes.

There were six of the comedians to perform, but each one was given only a relatively small spot of some five to six minutes and it was very difficult for a comedian to establish a presence in such a short time, but the audience loved them and Charlie's national success was assured.

The producer and director were extremely strict and each performance had to be vetted and scrupulously timed. The material was also checked to ensure that none of the jokes would offend the Royal Family. It was an extremely difficult show to stage, with so many artistes and with just the one rehearsal, but on the night it went like clockwork.

The majority of the performers were all incredibly nervous, especially the ones who had not previously appeared on a Royal Variety Show but Charlie took it all in his stride, believing it to be just another audience and when the spotlights were on, he could not see further than the first five rows and the royal box could not be seen at all. It was impossible for the artistes to see whether the Royal Party were enjoying their performance or not which was a bonus, because it would certainly have made them even more nervous.

The comedians shared one dressing-room and the conditions were cramped to say the very least, but the highlight of the show was the introduction to the Royal Family in the wings afterwards. Charlie remembers the meeting well and he spoke to both the Queen and Prince Philip. The Queen asked him how they all managed to understand each other being from different counties with different dialects. Charlie pointed out that he was working with his colleagues on a very regular basis and they soon got used to each other's accents, but he also pointed out to the Queen that she wasn't speaking to Yorkshire folk every day, so it was less of a problem for him.

Charlie asked Prince Philip for his autograph. Surprised by the request, Prince Philip turned to his aide and said, "I say, what do you think of this? We've got a right one here." He laughed, shook hands with Charlie and then moved on to Mike Reid. Charlie did not get his autograph, but then Prince Philip did not get Charlie's either.

Charlie remembers the show as a great occasion. The money was 'crap' but the performance gave him a high profile and helped to keep the money rolling in. There were those artistes in show-business who allowed the money to go to their heads and fortunes were gambled away by those who were incapable of coming to terms with the income which national stardom afforded. Charlie was as careful as ever, working as though it would be his last week in the business with no future income assured. He was extremely careful with his money, spending when only necessary and conserving and saving just in case the bubble burst.

Television exposure placed him in the mainstream of the hierarchy of entertainers and wherever Charlie went he was either guest star or top of the bill. Three television 'Specials' followed, two for Granada and one for the BBC in which Charlie was the star of the show and he introduced such special guests as Sacha Distel and

Brenda Arnau.

In the summer of 1973 he began a fifteen week summer season at the Floral Hall, Scarborough, for Duggie Chapman. The show included the highly entertaining Morton Fraser Harmonica Rascals, David and Marion Delmore, the ventriloquist Dawson Chance and Freddie Garrity of Freddie and the Dreamers fame. The first twelve weeks of the season were sold out within days of the tickets being placed on sale, and the final three weeks had queues of disappointed punters being turned away. The show broke all records and remains the highest selling season at that theatre of all time.

The band had ten musicians – different from the one keyboard synthesiser and drums player of today. There were twelve dancers and with full houses and good bar and programme sales a large cast could be supported.

There were twelve shows each week, two each day with the first at 6pm and the second house at 8.15pm. Sunday was left free but the acts simply moved venues to another resort for two Sunday Specials. On occasions Charlie would have to squeeze in a late-night cabaret to 'keep his eye in' so it was a hectic and nomadic lifestyle, prone to an excess of travelling and a surfeit of fatigue.

The Command performance had made a lasting impression on the Royals, and later that year Charlie was invited to appear at Windsor Castle - a far cry from the Royston Workingmen's Club!

"The M.C. wasn't wearing a cloth cap and I still didn't get Prince Philip's autograph, but then he didn't get mine either."

After the show Stanley Joseph contacted Charlie and offered him a job with a difference. He was to appear in a British made feature film called 'Man at the Top' with Kenneth Haigh, which would involve a week's shooting at the Pinewood studios in London. Charlie was to play the part of an irate father who was having trouble with his teenage daughter, a part played by a black 'Geordie' actress Angela Browne.

At the time of the filming, Charlie was appearing in late-night cabaret at the Fiesta Club in Sheffield and the schedule was tight. He would perform in Sheffield and then travel to London in the early hours of the morning ready for an early start. Sleep was confined to the car journeys and the back seat of the car whilst one of his friends endured the monotony of travelling to and fro along the M1. If anyone thought Charlie had an easy life, think again.

The following year Charlie was topping the bill for producer Duggie Chapman in *Snow White and the Seven Dwarfs* in Barnsley.

All was well with the cast until one of the dwarfs admitted a liaison with the wardrobe mistress which led to a pregnancy and no-one knew quite how to deal with the development. The event seemed to weigh heavily upon the dwarf's mind and he found himself embroiled in a web of deceit more colloquially know as the 'eternal triangle'.

He found solace in drink and within a very short time became reliant upon heavy intakes of alcohol so that he would be drunk during the performances, causing him to forget his lines and turning him into a thoroughly obnoxious character. His behaviour became intolerable, to the extent that Duggie had no alternative but to cancel his contract.

On the dwarf's final performance, he had to contend with the effects of a full afternoon's drinking together with his matrimonial difficulties and his pending unemployment. At the end of the show he had seized some of the pantomime merchandise, such as programmes and various gifts that parents were able to buy for their children, and he started flinging them into the audience.

Unfortunately the microphone managed to pick up the narrative and the children looked on in awe as the dwarf hurled expletive after expletive in the direction of Duggie Chapman and Charlie Williams, who were the two most prominent people concerned with the pantomime.

It was a tradition for the cast to shout Christmas greetings to the audience at the end of the show with the famous Christmas melody 'Jingle Bells' playing in the background. The cast took their bows and shouted their farewells. "Merry Christmas" shouted the cast, waving furiously as the audience waved back but the poisoned dwarf was intent on spoiling the finale, so he weaved between the cast adding shouts of his own into the microphones whilst the band played on. The comments were of varied content both from the cast and the dwarf.

"Merry Christmas!" "Happy New Year!"

"Piss off you 'orrible little bastards!"

"Have a good time!" "Happy New Year!"

"Duggie Chapman is a twat!"

"Merry Christmas everyone!"

"Bollocks!"

As the curtain fell, so did the dwarf. It is not a matter of record as to how that happened but it was the dwarf's last performance with the Duggie Chapman Company!

In the early 1970's Charlie was approached by the record

producer Ron Randall who was working with Columbia/EMI Records Limited. He had seen Charlie at the London Palladium and had heard him singing.

Ron took the view that he could utilise Charlie's popularity by releasing a long-playing record and he contacted Stanley and Michael Joseph in connection with the venture and the proposition was put to him. He remembers the conversation well. Ron made the opening remark,

"I didn't know you could sing."

To which Charlie replied,

"Neither did I!"

Charlie had never considered making a record, although singing was a small but integral part of his act. He liked the idea and agreed that he would go into the studio, but making a record involved the input of a great deal of time and effort.

The difficulty lay in Charlie's availability or lack of it since he was busier than ever and it was virtually impossible to arrange a sustained period at the studios, particularly in London. The record took some months to prepare and comprised eleven songs which all suited Charlie's voice and included standards such as *Walking My Baby Back Home, Little Things Mean a Lot, I Can't Stop Loving You* etc. The orchestra was arranged and conducted by Jeremy Lubbock and the vocal accompaniment was provided by the Mike Sammes Singers. The recording was undertaken at Chappel's Studios in London and the L.P. was released on the Columbia label by EMI Records Limited. It was entitled *'You Can't Help Liking...Charlie Williams'*.

On the record cover, it is very interesting to note a small

comment in the top right-hand corner which is assumed to be for the use of record shops to decide which category to place this record in. It simply says, 'File under popular...male vocal'. The famous disc-jockey Peter Murray wrote the narrative for the record cover, which included the words '......whether you see him on television, on stage or walking down the street, he's Charlie Williams, the personality-endowed Yorkshire comedian who first came into the nation's homes and hearts through Granada's highly successful television series *The Comedians*, and you really can't help liking him'. The record enjoyed considerable success.

In 1977/78 Charlie was appearing in the famous Pantomime *Dick Whittington*, at the Billingham Civic, which venue was a considerable contrast from the London Palladium, but it was a good season with an extremely partisan audience who understood and empathised with every inflection of voice and every comic line which he delivered.

The plot of the pantomime was traditional in that he was the comic hero with whom the audience found an affinity and there was the inevitable vulnerable female lead who was always persecuted by the villain for whom the audience could feel pure unadulterated hatred.

Whilst the plots do vary, essentially it is the same storyline and in this particular case the heroine was being persecuted by a wicked baron who was demanding payment of his rent. The heroine had been warned that unless the rent was paid, both she and her aged father would be cast out into the street.

The narrative of the pantomime had been set out with fundamental clarity, such as to leave the audience in absolutely no doubt that the baron was evil and the heroine was forlorn and desperate.

The cast developed the script, leaving in lines which gained merit and leaving out those which didn't, and after three or four weeks of the run and particularly after the Christmas festivities, post-Christmas blues had affected the audiences.

The quietest day was Wednesday and there was usually a matinee which was reserved for schools. One school from the locality brought eighty or so pupils, aged between seven and eleven. It was a school which will remain nameless, and had a considerable reputation for being downright hard. Some of the kids played conkers with hammers and even the local Samaritans were ex-directory.

If they had an Achilles heel it was the sympathy they felt for an unfortunate young woman, and the heroine played her part with such sincerity that it moved even the little hard men from the hardest of junior schools.

There was a part in the script where the heroine had to appeal to the audience to gain their sympathy.

"Oh, boys and girls, the wicked baron is going to take my house and throw me and my father into the street if I cannot pay the rent."

The audience favoured them with receptive sounds of 'oohs' and 'aahs'.

"I cannot pay my rent, boys and girls, so he will throw me out into the street."

The audience grew increasingly concerned and the oohs and aahs grew louder.

"He is coming tonight boys and girls for the rent, and I do not have it."

Even louder oohs and aahs rang around the auditorium and the cast made an excellent job of lulling the younger members of the audience into the belief that the pantomime was for real.

This was the point where Charlie as the comic male lead had to make his entrance and his cue were the words announced for the third time, "What shall I tell him?"

The heroine realised that she had the audience in her grip and she gave full vent to her pleas.

"What shall I tell him boys and girls?" she said as she looked to the left side of the audience.

"What shall I tell him boys and girls?" as she looked to the right side of the audience.

"What shall I tell him boys and girls?" she implored to the circle, and with that a little boy from the aforementioned school, with a crew-cut, a hair lip and a running nose stepped into the aisle and shouted with incredible vigour,

"Tell him to fuck off!"

Charlie had made his entrance just as the little boy had made his riposte and was unable to keep his composure. He burst into a fit of laughter to be joined by the heroine and then the wicked baron himself who had entered stage left. The band were next and then the lighting and sound engineers. The audience joined in and for a matter of some minutes the entire gathering was seized in the grip of hilarity.

Comedy is not always an enjoyable work experience. Indeed it is a profession of extremes, but there are occasions which stand out in the memory more than others and the incident at the Billingham Civic was one which neither Charlie nor the cast and crew would ever forget.

As a result of Charlie's endeavours, he had attracted a great deal of respect from club owners who often called upon him when they had been let down by another artiste. Charlie would always turn out if he could and in the 1970's he was called upon to help out at the popular venue, the Fiesta Club in Sheffield.

The American singing star Dionne Warwick had been booked to appear for two Saturday shows but unfortunately the advance bookings were nowhere near as good as expected and consequently Miss Warwick decided not to appear. The audiences were concentrated into one show and Charlie was called in at very short notice to replace her. It meant doing his other show a little earlier than was intended and then a high speed chase to Sheffield for the cabaret appearance.

The cancellation was noted in the newspapers and refunds were offered, but to Charlie's credit only twelve people made a claim. When he was introduced to the audience, his opening line was,

"Same colour, different sex!"

Apparently his comic rendition of 'Do you know the way to San Jose?' went down extremely well, although he had to wear a very tight jock-strap to help him hit the high notes!

Charlie kept performing at all the big theatres and clubs and he was never more popular than at Batley Variety Club, with whom his name had become synonymous. The owner was one James Corrigan, a member of the famous fairground and show-people family who had brought some of the country's biggest stars to Batley, but the most popular of all was Charlie Williams who was voted 'King of Batley' for being the favourite act.

"It was a great honour and I was thrilled to be chosen. I was given a crown and a robe and some witty bugger gave me a spear. I held the crown and robe for a full year, but I kept the spear!"

Charlie remembers one particular engagement when Corrigan booked him for a full week, but at the time he was still under contract to Granada with *The Comedians* and they held an option, which meant that they had first call upon Charlie's services. The booking was taken on the basis that if he was booked elsewhere under the option he would have to give up the week's work at Batley.

In the event, Charlie was given a pre-panto contract in Peterborough which he had no option but to accept. Corrigan, on the other hand, had different ideas since he had already prepared the advance advertising and consequently suggested to Charlie that he did both the Peterborough concerts and his week at Batley. Charlie was not afraid of hard work but the logistics of it did not stack up. Corrigan was undeterred and promised to sort out the rather complicated question of the travelling arrangements.

"It's a simple matter," said Corrigan, ever the optimist. "I'll arrange for a helicopter to fly you from Peterborough to Batley."

Unfortunately helicopters were not allowed to make the journey at night so Corrigan had to think again.

The Peterborough show finished at 9.50pm and Charlie was due on stage at Batley at 11.15pm which would allow only one hour twenty-five minutes from door to door. Corrigan then came up with a solution by placing his Rolls Royce at Charlie's disposal.

The plan was that Charlie would drive to Batley in the afternoon and then a driver would take him in the Rolls to the theatre in Peterborough. When the show had finished, Charlie would sit in the back of the car and relax whilst the especially chosen driver then raced back to Batley. Charlie kept his eyes firmly closed on the return journey.

"What the eye didn't see................"

Corrigan's plan worked and as ever he got his way, but then Corrigan usually did.

"I liked Corrigan. He was straight John Bull easy to talk to. He would always be able to talk himself out of a crisis and he never gave in, but despite all that he was fair and he never let me down. As far as I was concerned, his word was his bond - and so was mine."

Chapter Fifteen

THE GOLDEN SHOT

It was not always beneficial for an artiste to be black but the 1970's brought about an era of being politically correct. Even the epitome of wholesome entertainment, *The Black and White Minstrel Show* did not remain unscathed. It was a small but interesting parallel with the McCarthy witch-hunts of the 50's and may have started with an incident at the Royal Variety Performance in 1967 when the top of the bill, Diana Ross would not go on until the Minstrels had left the stage. Apparently no-one questioned it. Race dominated the political agenda.

In the new climate of cultural sensitivity the long-running *Black and White Minstrel Show* was banned from the screen. An announcement from a BBC spokesman said,

"The show cannot be seen on television again because it would probably be offensive to the ethnic minority of Britain."

The Black and White Minstrels were consigned to the summer shows and in the 1970's they were headlining in summer season in Scarborough, but they were still immensely popular with audiences and bookings were good.

Charlie was a regular in Scarborough and he was asked to appear as guest star with The Minstrels, who were still smarting from their television exile when Charlie turned up. The first point of discussion was the politically correct attitude.   Charlie was asked for his opinion and he gave it in his customary disarming way,

"If they think I'm whiting up they can bugger off!"

Charlie had made his point and highlighted the 'knee jerk' reaction to an age old problem which would never be solved by simple exclusion from television.

The show was a success and the public loved it and Charlie's drawing of attention to the peculiar rationale of being politically correct got the greatest laugh of all.   Of course he made a good living by being politically incorrect, but a better financial prospect was on the horizon.

Charlie was a much sought-after artiste and on the strength of *The Comedians,* the producer of the programme *The Golden Shot* approached Stanley and Michael Joseph and suggested that he take over the role of compere from Norman Vaughan.

The producer liked Charlie's style and the rapport he created with the audience and felt that he would be an ideal replacement.

Stanley Joseph was approached and discussed the project. Charlie was working seven nights a week and only had Sunday mornings and afternoons off, although travelling robbed him of the afternoon.   *The Golden Shot* was filmed on Sundays and the fee was £750 per show which by the standards of the day was a substantial sum.

Charlie was unsure what to do.   On the one hand he was working very hard and needed to spend some time with his family, but on the other he was anxious to add security to their lives.   He was not so naïve as to think he would stay at the top of the tree for ever, so he had a difficult decision to make and he was given a month to

Charlie at 5 years of age.

Charlie and friends from Upton Colliery, circa 1953.

A spot-the-ball contest in the Doncaster Rovers v Leyton Orient match in 1956, with Harry Gregg then keeping goal for Rovers, and Orient centre forward Tom Johnstone. Barratt's Photo Press Ltd.

Playing his first season at Doncaster Rovers.

Doncaster Rovers 1st team 1955/56 including the Ireland international goalkeeper Harry Gregg and Charlie's friend Alick Jeffrey (bottom row, second left).

All Stars football team featuring former professional players who played for charity, circa 1960's.

Charlie and Alick Jeffrey at the beginning of his show business career, 1958.

Charlie and Janice on their wedding day.

Charlie featured with Lord Delfont and Norman Collier at the London Palladium, 1972.

Charlie with fellow comedians Duncan Norvelle, Billy Pearce, Tommy Cannon and Bobby Ball.

This was the line-up for the very first transmission of The Comedians. *Front row, from the left: Paul Melba, Mike Coyne myself and Bernard Manning. Back row: George Roper, Ken Goodwin, Duggie Brown and Frank Carson.*

Granada Television

With Her Majesty The Queen at the Royal Variety Command Performance, 1972, also pictured Joss White and Mike Reid.

'Charlie Williams — This Is Your Life!' That's me with the spear. The rest of the folks, from the left, are: Duggie Brown, my cousin Dennis Bedford, Freddie Trueman, cousins Ralph and George Bedford, Frank Carson, Eamonn Andrews, Steve Faye, Johnny Hamp, producer of The Comedians, and George Roper.

Thames Television

Charlie and Janice pictured with the American recording artistes "The Drifters."

Charlie, Janice and Shirley Bassey.

Charlie with Julie Lockwood and Mike Williams of Yorkshire Television filming an interview for Calendar 1998.

Neil Crossland, Charlie and Steve Smith (author).

JIMMY KILKENNY (Right-half). Played his first game for the Rovers against Bristol City last Saturday, and gave an impressive display. This 20-years old player has just completed his national service. He is a product of the Rovers' "nursery" in the north-east, and joined the Belle Vue club from Anfield Plain. A bright future is predicted for this young player.

CHARLIE WILLIAMS (Centre-half). This coloured pivot is a great favourite at Belle Vue, where his acrobatic antics please the crowd. Charlie successfully held Bedford Jezzard, England's centre-forward last week, and his speed and knack of being in time certainly have served his side well.

JACK TEASDALE (Left-half). One of the most improved players in the Belle Vue side. Another native of Rossington, who has graduated through the Rovers' junior teams. Present form suggests representative honours before long. Tackles hard and well and will be a top-class wing-half when his ball distribution improves.

JOHNNY MOONEY (Outside-right). A Scot signed by the Rovers from Hamilton Academicals three seasons ago, and a player who at first never seemed clear of injuries. Has overcome his troubles and is, without doubt, one of the best wingers in football to-day. Gets goals because of his persistence and because of his intelligent anticipation.

ALICK JEFFREY (Inside-right). Although only 16 years of age is being talked about as one of the best players in the post-war era. Already holds schoolboy, junior, intermediate and amateur international caps, and seems destined for more honours. Went with Great Britain's Olympic Games team to Bulgaria recently.

EDDIE McMORRAN (Centre-forward). One of the best known names in soccer. Eddie may leave the Rovers before long as the club is open to receive offers for this genial Irishman who has had a long experience with Manchester City, Leeds United and Barnsley. Would be a very useful asset to many clubs, although Doncaster would be loath to let such a loyal servant go.

BERT TINDILL (Inside-left). The club's utility player who, although still in his twenties, is one of the longest serving players. Has a terrific shot in either foot, and is a goal-maker and a goal getter. A native of South Yorkshire who is admired by many other League clubs.

GEOFF WALKER (Outside-left). Gave his best display against Fulham since he went to Doncaster from Middlesbrough. A grand player to watch and has been aptly named "twinkle-feet". Can pin-point centres to a foot or so of where he wants them to drop, and can also score with a tremendous left-foot drive. Started his Soccer career with Bradford Park Avenue at 15 years of age.

Pen portrait taken from Leeds United football match progamme.

Sirree! **Jubil**

su

you'll find it suit

BREWED AND BOTTLED BY HOPE &

SHEFFIELD WEDNESDAY
Blue & White Striped Shirts, Black Knickers

Dave McINTOSH

Ron STANIFORTH [2]		Norman CURTIS [3]
Don GIBSON [4]	Don McEVOY [5]	Ralph O'DONNELL [6]
Albert QUIXALL [8]		Redfern FROGGATT [10]
Alan FINNEY [7]	Roy SHINER [9]	Albert BROADBENT [11]

Referee :	WILL SEE	Linesmen :
P. F. POWER, York.	YOU ON 21st JANUARY AT 2.45 p.m.	R. C. BLADON, Burton-on-Trent (Red Flag) : J. B. COLEMAN, Cheshire (Yellow Flag).

Ron WALKER [11]	Eddie McMORRAN [9]	John MOONEY [7]
Bert TINDILL [10]		Alick JEFFREY [8]
Jack TEASDALE [6]	Charlie WILLIAMS [5]	James KILKENNY [4]
Paddy GAVIN [8]		Brian MAKEPEACE [2]

Ken HARDWICK

DONCASTER ROVERS
White Shirts with Red Collars, Black Knickers

For your **FAMILY** c

THE BAKERS of the **BEST**

★ PLACE YOUR ORDER WITH YOUR GROCER

its **Guns**

its **Goo**

Advertising Rights acquired by " Sports P

Team sheets, Sheffield Wednesday v Rovers, 14/1/56.

Charlie's first promotional photograph, with the kind permission of Eric Todd.

Charlie doing the Can-Can at the Clubland awards ceremony, by kind permission of Eric Todd.

Charlie in typical pose.

Charlie at the record breaking summer season at the Scarborough Floral Hall.

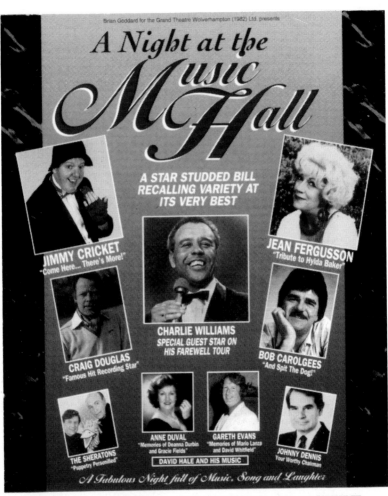

A Night at the Music Hall, Charlie's farewell tour.

Clubscene 1

Charlie finally set to hang up his boots

CHARLIE Williams, the popular comedian, is to retire after spending the last 24 years in the forefront of Yorkshire comedy.

Last week Charlie told me he is to embark on a Twilight Tour, commencing on Friday, January 20, at Keresforth Hall, and taking in ten to 12 venues, which will bring down the curtain on a glittering career.

Charlie (67), came into showbusiness when his football career ended.

He tried working the clubs as a singer with another footballer Alec Jeffries, but this wasn't a success.

He then took to comedy and found he could make people laugh, although still finding the going very difficult.

Success started for Charlie on May 18, 1970, when he was selected to appear in the Yorkshire Clubland Command Performance.

He was an instant success, getting a standing ovation from one of the largest crowds ever seen at Batley Variety Club and was crowned 'King of Batley.'

A member of the audience was Johnny Hamp, who later produced *The Comedians.*

That week Charlie was invited to join ATS Agency (Leeds) and from then his career took off as he starred in *The Comedians*, played a season at the London Palladium and worked all the top carbaret venues in the country.

In the spring of 1970 I asked him if he would be interested in appearing in a command preview.

He replied: "No one wants to know me, a black comedian with a Barnsley accent."

He did appear, got through to the final and the rest is history.

Here was a person who was always willing to help others and available for charity shows.

I wish him well on his retirement and many happy years golfing.

KIMBERWORTH PARK AND WINGFIELD SOCIAL CLUB

The Best Entertainment In South Yorkshire

TELEPHONE ROTHERHAM 551577

SATURDAY, JANUARY 14th
TOP ACT FROM BLACKPOOL
NOW HEAR THIS
BE EARLY!
SUNDAY, JANUARY 15th
BRILLIANT TRIO IN CLUBLAND
TRI-STAR
BOTH SHOWS NOT TO BE MISSED

TUESDAY, WEDNESDAY
CLUB ACTIVITIES
All artistes to be on call for 7.30 and ready for work otherwise there will be a cut in their fee.
Children's room must be used on concerts night and is now open on Sunday dinner

MEMBERS AND AFFILIATED MEMBERS ONLY.

The Flamingo Room and Kingfisher Restaurant
KERESFORTH HALL

EASTWOOD VIEW WMC
FITZWILLIAM ROAD, ROTHERHAM
SATURDAY, JANUARY 14th
JAGGED EDGE

ROTHERHAM TRANSPORT CLUB
UNION STREET. PHONE 551478
SATURDAY, JANUARY 14th—
BILLION

Rotherham Trades Club
Telephone Rotherham 364975.
Concert Sec S. MANDERSON
DAVID ALLEN Organ, DAVID Drums

FRIDAY, JANUARY 13th—
FAMILY NIGHT
BRING YOUR FAMILY TO HEAR
TOP CLUBLAND DUO
FLYING COLOURS
PLUS USUAL CLUB ACTIVITIES

SATURDAY, JANUARY 14th—
THE FABULOUS
LINACRES
SUNDAY, JANUARY 15th—
NOON ONLY
2 FOR THE BOYS
NIGHT ONLY
DENE AND SPATE
(STAR DUO)
MONDAY, JANUARY 16th—
STAR VOCALIST
ROBERT CRAIG
THURSDAY, JANUARY 19th—
SONGS FROM
JOAN

Charlie's announcement of retirement, as recorded in the Rotherham Advertiser, 13th January 1995.

Charlie at home in retirement.

Neil Crossland, Charlie, Alan Oliver and the Author,
Lifetime Achievement Award, July 1998.

consider the offer. The terms of the contract were simple: a six month term of working twenty-six Sundays, with an option to extend for a further twenty-six shows at the expiry of the first contract.

Unlike *The Comedians* at which opportunity Charlie had jumped immediately, this was a different proposition. He had been used to a stand-up comedy routine aimed directly at an audience so that he was working solo, entirely dependent upon his material and his audience's reaction. *The Golden Shot* was different; it was in the nature of a game show with regular exchanges with contestants and for part of the programme he had to work from a script.

Charlie deliberated for the whole of the month but the lure of the money proved too much for him and he accepted the contract. With the benefit of hindsight, he feels he made the wrong decision.

The series was filmed in ATV's Birmingham studio before a live audience on Sunday afternoons following one rehearsal earlier in the day. It was peak viewing on a Sunday afternoon with an audience of many millions and the pressure was intense.

The cast comprised of Ann Aston, a bubbly blond with an infectious personality which suited her role as hostess extremely well, and who had been with the series for some time.

The other member was 'Bernie the Bolt', the technician who guided a studio crossbow onto a series of targets. He was in a control room out of sight and followed the contestant's instructions as to directing the weapon to it's target. Time limits were imposed to add excitement to the proceedings and the contestants were able to win substantial sums of money.

Charlie had difficulties settling. He was out of character, something he realised after the first show. The programme was extremely popular but the critics were less than enthusiastic about his handling of the show. Regrettably Charlie received little or no assistance from the production team, something which he feels played a large part in him deciding not to exercise his option to accept the six month renewal.

He completed his contract and the producer was happy with the programme, but despite the executives' overtures Charlie decided against the renewal and his brief sojourn with the programme was over. If there was any regret in Charlie's career it was being involved with *The Golden Shot.*

The sporting arena was to make a welcome return to Charlie's life, when in 1976 he was approached by Barnsley Football Club and was asked to join the Board of Directors. He accepted the offer at a time when Barnsley were struggling in the old fourth division of the Football League and he gave to the club the benefit of his name and considerable knowledge of football and players, for which he received a free season ticket and a return to the game he loved.

The Board were ambitious and one of the first decisions in which Charlie played a part was to bring the Leeds United and England International, Alan Clarke, to Oakwell as player-manager. Clarke was an immediate success and the season saw promotion to Division Three but unfortunately for Barnsley, Leeds United took Clarke back to manage their team, only for him to return some time later when he fell out of favour with the First Division side.

Charlie's directorship lasted for eight years, ending with his resignation in 1984, an action prompted by his dislike of 'player power'. He felt that finance had become the focal point of the game and players' wages and terms dominated the agenda. He believes that the money which is claimed by some players in today's game is immoral. It is a view not borne out of the regrets of an old player who did not achieve the dizzy heights of financial security, but more of a man who held the old traditions of the game at heart. The times were changing and Charlie would not compromise his beliefs, so he and two other directors left the boardroom for the last time, returning only as a guest. He has retained stand tickets ever since.

Charlie maintained his close ties with sport by pursuing another ball game, a little more sedate than football. Golf has always been one of Charlie's passions and he would take his clubs with him wherever he was working just in case he could snatch an hour's play. His game was of a reasonable standard and he was often invited to play at Pro-Am Tournaments, being a regular guest at the Les Dawson Classic held every summer at Lytham St Annes.

Charlie had met Les in the late sixties when they were both working the northern club scene and they had become friends, so it was a pleasurable experience for them both to get together and play golf. The evening of the tournament was spent in a hotel and when Les spotted Charlie's entrance, he would go to the piano and play a chorus of *'Old Man River'*, much to the amusement of everybody present.

Charlie had the highest regard for Les, whom he considered to be one of the country's greatest funnymen.

"Les had a fantastic vocabulary which he used to great effect in his material. He was also a good musician and accomplished writer, but most of all, he was a nice bloke and great fun to be with."

Tragically Les died too early but not before he had left a considerable legacy for posterity in the form of recordings of his work and his books.

Morecambe and Wise were also great favourites of his with talent unsurpassed by any of the modern comedians, although of the present day stars Charlie admires Des O'Connor and Billy Connolly.

Chapter Sixteen

The 80's

The 1980's began much as the 1970's left off, with Charlie working seven days a week. His fame had taken him to the four corners of the country and television exposure had made him a national star, whose orbit now encompassed the theatres of the south of England and the studios of national television, light years from the South Yorkshire Workingmen's Clubs.

It was said that Charlie did more for the 'regionalised comedian' than anyone else. Televised humour tended to emanate from the London area, but *The Comedians* broke the mould and with acts like Charlie Williams, Ken Goodwin and Colin Crompton the era of the comedian with a northern accent was at its height. The stars of *The Comedians* were featured in other successful television shows including the Wheeltappers' and Shunters' Social Club, with regulars Colin Crompton and Bernard Manning playing host to a number of northern artistes in a workingmen's club type setting.

Charlie continued to make television appearances and, with the considerable assistance of Stanley and Michael Joseph, he continued to perform at high quality venues throughout the country. Michael Joseph remembers the 1980's with affection,

"He was our easiest artiste to book. Everyone wanted Charlie Williams and everyone liked him."

The inevitable summer season, which occupied three to four months, gave way to a short concert and cabaret season before pantomime and then the whole process repeated itself.

Blackpool was one of his favourite venues, particularly for the summer season and in the summer of 1987 he was top of the bill at the South Pier Theatre. It was a good engagement of some ten weeks and he was sharing the bill with an old friend, the great stand-up comedian Norman Collier. Charlie remembers that season particularly well, not least because of Mr Collier's sense of fun. The opening weekend meant that the stars and some of the guests of the show had to drive along in an open-top bus through the centre of Blackpool and along the promenade to advertise the show. The first of such journeys found them accompanied by the Lord Mayor and his wife, an occasion which the dignitaries treated very seriously, but which unfortunately Mr Collier did not. Norman used it as an excuse for a laugh.

There was a man with a megaphone at the front of the bus, shouting out the advertising spiel and it attracted a great deal of attention both from the promenade and on the beach nearby.

"Roll up, roll up! Come and see Charlie Williams and Norman Collier in the funniest show in Blackpool. Full of songs and laughter, this is a show not to be missed - Roll up, roll up! Come and see ....etc etc"

Charlie and Norman had to sit at the front on the top deck of the bus, waving to passers-by and throwing sweets for the children which Norman found quite acceptable for the first twenty minutes, but then becoming a little bored by the whole thing hit upon the idea of taking over the loudspeaker and doing some of the advertising himself. However the narrative was not quite the same as that of his colleague as he announced,

"Roll up, roll up!   Come and see Charlie Williams and the farting kangaroo.   Was it the fart that made him jump, or the jump that made him fart!   Roll up, Roll up. Come and see for yourselves.   Charlie Williams and the farting kangaroo."

The Lord Mayor was highly amused but his lady Mayoress was not impressed as she noted some of her afternoon tea-party friends gathered on the promenade waiting for a taxi.   She hung her head in shame when Norman continued,

"Roll up, roll up!   Come and see the farting kangaroo!"

The Lady Mayoress need not have been so upset, Norman wasn't referring to her.

It was a great season and was to be one of many spent at that grand old theatre.   There were twelve shows each week and Sundays were occupied with 'specials' usually at another coastal resort.   Inevitably the night-club scene called upon Charlie's services and late-night performances left him drained, but the life-blood was the audience and their reaction provided the adrenalin which overcame the weariness.

Norman recalls those days very well,

"Charlie was easy to work with.   There was no pretension about him.   He was just a normal and nice fellow.   Even when he became successful he didn't alter, he was the same old Charlie with no edge to him.   I have seen people change with success and not for the better, but not him."

Charlie and Norman enjoyed each other's company and they found an affinity in golf when they would share a round and trade new jokes. Norman continued,

"Charlie always used to tell me how he liked hitting white balls. I always wondered what he meant."

Norman relished the working relationship which extended over many years and from time to time they work together, when Norman claims he gets his jokes back!

The impression may be that Charlie never learned to deal with failure; but not all of his endeavours were successful and one of his disappointments was a night-club venture in which he had become involved in the early 1980's. Premises on Barber Street at Hoyland, Barnsley, formerly known as the Barber Street Workingmen's Club had been empty for some time. They belonged to a local brewery and were available for rent so Charlie decided to take over the lease of the premises and open his own night-club. The club was called 'Charlies' and opened in 1980 managed by his daughter Beverley and it was intended that he would appear as often as he could when his normal cabaret work was over. Unfortunately he was not always in the immediate area and it was not possible for him to appear as regularly as he would have liked.

The club was relatively small with a capacity of only two hundred and fifty people and a full house was needed to put the club into profit. It may have seemed that being a local celebrity would have been an advantage, but Bernard Manning had some advice for Charlie which he now accepts he should have taken. Manning advised him against opening a club in the district where he lived because it would involve too many complimentary tickets, and being local it would have the unusual effect of limiting the amount of patronage that he could expect.

Unfortunately after two years the writing was on the wall that the club was not going to be successful and consequently, albeit reluctantly, Charlie sold out. He does not dwell on the subject but just recalls that it was not the wisest of moves and simply smiles when he says,

"Well, it didn't make a profit."

Despite overtures from other quarters, it was the last business venture of its type that Charlie was to undertake. Charlie is philosophical about the club, but he puts the venture down to experience, never being one to dwell on the past and he was most certainly never one to waste money. If anything, it helped Charlie to realise his true forte, which was in performing and so that summer he concentrated on his season at the coast.

Robin Colvill is a member of the great comedy showgroup The Grumbleweeds, and he appeared on many summer seasons with Charlie in Blackpool. He recalls how professional Charlie was in his approach to his act,

"We would always be having a laugh and got up to all sorts of tricks and behaviour, but despite Charlie's reputation as a comedian, he was so extremely focused on his act that he tended to have his own way of dealing with stress. He would sit quietly in his dressing-room mulling over what he was going to do and say, even ran through the words of his songs. He combated stress with professionalism and only when his performance was finished, did he tend to relax. We on the other hand would rub Fiery Jack into other members of our group's jock-straps and wait for the result when we were on stage. There was never a dull moment, particularly with the Fiery Jack! The tendency to scratch and sit in a bowl of ice-cold water was overwhelming."

If Charlie had a choice, he much preferred to perform to a live audience in cabaret than any other medium, but he enjoyed the odd appearance on radio. It was a useful vehicle to advertise forthcoming shows and pantomimes, so he was never averse to using the opportunity to his own advantage, so that the radio station got the services of a big star and Charlie got to advertise for free. Everyone was happy.

Live radio can be very exciting because there is no prospect of a producer editing the interview and cutting-out any pieces which have been controversial, which is why so many radio producers have ulcers.

Charlie was interviewed one day, prior to opening in a summer season, by a then well-known presenter who was moving towards the end of his career. It was the day before the start of the presenter's annual leave and he was desperately keen to get away to start his holiday. Charlie on the other hand was as fresh as a daisy, about to start a summer season and needed to promote the show as much as possible.

It was the start of the new innovation of radio 'phone-ins', when people were encouraged to speak to the guest of the day and ask questions. It allowed comedians such as Charlie to display their talents of ad-libbing and the formula appealed to the listeners. The radio now adopts a method of screening so that they have an idea of what is going to be said but on this occasion one caller was allowed to slip through the net who really didn't have a question at all, but just wanted to explain a bereavement to a presenter with whom she felt an affinity.

The interview had gone extremely well, until the unfortunate Marge was put through to Charlie, live over the airwaves. The presenter made a formal introduction of the caller and then continued:

Presenter: "You're through to Charlie now Marge. What's your question?"

Marge: "Hello Charlie."

Charlie: "Hello Marge.   Are you alreight my flower?"

Mavis: "I am Charlie, although I'm very sad."

Charlie: "Oh dear, why is that Marge?"

Marge: "Well, my husband Jack and me love your act."

Charlie: "Thank you my flower, it's very nice of you to say so..........."

Charlie was interrupted.

Marge: "In fact, we've seen you many times and we always watch your programme, The Comedians."

Charlie: "Thank you my flower, that's very nice..........."

Marge interrupted again.

Marge: "Ay, my husband Jack thought you were the best comedian going."

Charlie: "Well, thank........"

Marge: "He died on Monday, but he's in our front room now in his coffin, the lid is off and people are coming to pay their respects, you know, they come just to say goodbye."

Charlie and the Presenter were taken aback, so Charlie tried to take charge of the situation.

Charlie: "I'm very sorry to hear that Marge."

Marge: "Aye, it's all right Charlie, he had a good life, he was eighty-five.   He looks so peaceful I just wanted you to know how much our Jack loved your act ...smashing!"

Charlie: "I'm deeply touched.   Thank you very much........."

Marge interrupted again.

Marge: "Aye, he's in his coffin in our front room and you'd be surprised how many people have come to pay their respects.   He was a right decent bloke our Jack."

Presenter: "Well Marge, we wonder if you would like to have a record played for....."

Marge interrupted yet again.

Marge: "Aye, sixty-two years we were married. It was a good marriage as well.   Aye, sixty two years!"

This time the Presenter interrupted.

Presenter: "Well Marge, would you like us to play a record for you and your Jack?   It's the very least we can do......."

He was interrupted again.

Marge: "Aye, sixty-two years we were married and never a cross word.   I was right lucky I was, right lucky.   Do you know.........?"

Presenter: "Marge, we would like to play a record especially for you and we're running out of time.   Have you any special request?"

Marge: "No.   Any record at all that's bright and

breezy, because we don't want it to be a sad occasion for our Jack. He's in our front room now and people are coming to see him. It's a real pleasure for people to come and pay their respects."

The Presenter faded Marge out and he decided to impose a break in the proceedings and play a record. He reached for a large pack of compact discs but unfortunately he had mislaid his glasses and he couldn't quite make out what each one said. He pointed the C.D. towards Charlie and gesticulated in questioning mode. Charlie mouthed the name, 'Clodagh Rogers'.

Presenter: "Right Marge, we have selected something bright and breezy by that wonderful singer, Clodagh Rogers and here she is to sing......er...... so here is a track from an LP by Clodagh Rogers, especially for Marge and her Jack.

The Presenter, Charlie and the Producer sat open-mouthed and in complete shock as Clodagh Rogers' opening words hit the airwaves.

Clodagh: "He's..... just..... a..... jack-in-the-box, a jack-in-a-box............"

Whilst the microphones were switched off, Charlie leaned across to the Presenter and simply said,

"Let's see thee get out of that one then! I like Clodagh Rogers though! Nice one that! Jack-in-a-box, very good that, I like that."

The Producer left the studio with tears flowing down his reddened cheeks!

Charlie found himself opening new supermarkets, appearing at presentations and making special appearances before setting off for his cabaret dates. It was not unusual to make three separate performances in one day, but it left a legacy of disharmony at home. There could be no doubt that over the years he had seen less and less of his family and despite the security that his hard work brought, his marriage began to fail. Audrey sought a life elsewhere and Mr & Mrs Williams were parted.

Despite the separation Charlie saw his children as often as he could. The stresses and the trauma of a broken marriage were difficult enough to deal with, without being involved in one of the most stressful professions of all, but inevitably Charlie took it all in his stride with his work providing a welcome relief. But there was a sad side to it all which the public did not see.

He would sit alone in his dressing-room and mull over the events of the day and what was happening in his life. At the time of the divorce he was trying to cope with a huge workload from the loneliness of a hotel room and finding it the most distressing time of his life. He was also parted from his children and this state of affairs had a profound effect upon him. He would reflect upon his troubles and worries knowing that only minutes later he was required on stage with the task of making people laugh. The audience had made a special effort to attend and in some cases had saved up their hard-earned money to buy tickets. They wouldn't really be interested in the artiste's problems. They had bought their ticket and they wanted to see the show. Audiences are also fickle, hence the uncertainty of show-business and in many ways such is its attraction for its artistes. Living on the edge, the taste of fear, providing the impetus that a performer needs to perform well. Complacency destroys a good act but Charlie was never complacent although he knew all about hardships. In short, he had been skint and the condition did not appeal to him but his marital difficulties were to re-introduce him to the condition.

His divorce provided the vehicle for yet a further conditioning of work and this was the only good thing to come out of it. The downside was the cost. The odd thing about divorce is that the question of fault has no bearing upon who got what.

Charlie had a full diary and commitments like that won't go away when you feel under the weather. Divorce is considered to be one of the highest points on the scales of stress, but the old maxim 'the show must go on' is ever present. The problem with the entertainment industry is that it is so very singular and as Charlie was 'the act', he was entirely dependent upon himself having no work-mates to whom he could turn to help him out. The bookings were in his name and they had to be honoured, whether he liked it or not. Unlike the N.C.B. the audience would not accept sick-notes, and in any event Charlie was not the sort of person to let anyone down. In many ways, he was able to bury himself in his work, which together with the huge amount of travelling, provided something of a distraction from all his problems.

The ramifications of an acrimonious divorce may make interesting reading for some, but beyond what has been said, it is not a phase in Charlie's life upon which he likes to dwell. Suffice it to say that eventually matters were resolved and Charlie's marriage was ended. Fortunately Charlie kept in touch with his children and he saw them whenever he could but Audrey later remarried and that chapter in Charlie's life was closed, some would say for the better.

The higher up the show-business ladder that Charlie travelled the bigger the stars with whom he came into contact. It was a delightful diversification because it allowed him to meet some of the other great comedians of the day and a particular favourite of Charlie's was Tommy Cooper whom he met in the early 70's. They became firm friends and when Cooper was in the Yorkshire area, he would either stay with him or at least share a meal.

Charlie remembers that Cooper was invariably late, a fault which never affected his work, but played havoc with his private life. Cooper also liked to drink to find a release from the never-ending pressures of travelling and performing.

Cooper was a great favourite in the Yorkshire cabaret scene and he made frequent visits to the Fiesta Club in Sheffield where he always received a great welcome and if Charlie was available, he would attend the show and stand in the wings and watch the great man work.

Cooper had a unique brand of humour and the ability to create laughter with just a facial expression. Charlie recalls Cooper's act:

"He didn't have to say anything to start me off, for my money he was perhaps one of the best comedians that we ever produced."

The other unusual thing about Cooper was that his material was peculiar to him and could not be stolen or re-worked in any other way by anyone else.

Most comedians' jokes do the rounds and are passed

from comic to comic, but with a visual type of humour such as Cooper's it was virtually impossible to copy; a test of greatness. Tommy Cooper's originality was an impressionist's dream, with the manic laughter and the ubiquitous fez. He would appear at Charlie's house, answering an invitation for dinner, usually late and more often than not, the worse for wear after drink. One of his party tricks was to hammer on the door and when it was opened he would fall flat on his face and remain there for what seemed an interminable period. He would then stand and compliment Charlie upon the sleeping arrangements.

Charlie said of him,

"Tommy was a great comic. He could make you laugh with just a look, he was one of my favourite comedians."

Chapter Seventeen

JANICE

Janice Greer was to become Charlie's second wife. She was born in the Midlands in 1944 and the circumstances surrounding her conception and birth were unusual to say the least. Her mother had married at eighteen years of age but in 1939 her husband went to war and she was not to see him again until 1945.

In 1943 her father came to Britain with the American army. He was a black G.I. and formed an association with Janice's mother. A relationship developed which resulted in the birth of a female child who was named Janice.

When Janice was eleven months old her 'stepfather' returned home to a hero's welcome and a coloured step-daughter he had never met. Janice was too young to remember what transpired, but some time later she was informed that her mother was forced to give her up and she was placed in a children's home. She was never to see her mother again, although there was to be a fleeting contact by telephone over fifty years later when Janice traced her and tried to arrange a meeting. Her mother declined the opportunity however, despite the overtures which had been made to talk her round.

Janice speaks of her life in the children's home with great affection. When she was two years old a sister who had been ordained into the Methodist faith came to the children's home in search of a candidate to make up a family group of ten children in a home at Harpenden.

Her name was Sister Ann and the concept of 'sisterhood' came from the National Children's Home which set up an order of carers. They were named 'sisters', were trained under the auspices of the Methodist Church and it was necessary to obtain two certificates to qualify. There were similarities between these sisters and sisters of the Catholic Church, but accent was on caring as opposed to religious devotion. In the early seventies they were paid the princely sum of thirteen pounds per month.

Each sister had charge of ten children but Sister Ann was one child short and became enamoured with Janice who was chosen from a class in a large children's home. She has no bitterness about being in the home, for she had as much attention as she would have gained anywhere else and believes that she had more material things than would have been on offer with the average family.

When Janice was nine years old, the sister in charge of her group left the home and was replaced by Sister Beaulah Walters who was to have a profound effect upon her young charge.

Sister Beaulah was young, keen and extremely devoted and Janice became extremely attached to her but at first Janice felt 'out of it'. She knew she was different and children being what children are, they could be extremely cruel so that the time soon came when she felt as though she had a handicap.

She remained with the N.C.H. until she was seventeen years old but if there was anything missing, it was that special relationship which exists between parents of the full blood and their child.

Her mentor was a man called Edward Shutt who was the governor of the home and was a kind and generous man who took Janice under his wing, treating her as if she was a child of his own. He encouraged her in her schooling and particularly in sport so perhaps he was the father figure that Janice had yearned for; her inspiration to succeed.

There was one interesting similarity with Charlie as she was the only black child in her school and she recalls that she was eleven before she became aware of colour prejudice. The teacher gave her a role as a class monitor and one of her duties was to ensure that all the desks were in a line and were neat and tidy. She recalled that one girl had moved her desk out of line but the teacher was fastidious and so was Janice, in her anxiety to please. As she moved one desk, the owner took exception which manifested itself in a stinging rebuke when she announced, "Leave my desk alone blackie." It was the first time that Janice had realised that the difference was thought important.

There was a fight and Janice gave a very good account of herself. She remembers talking through the incident with Mr Shutt, who realised it was time to deal with something which could be a problem, particularly in later life.

Janice admits that it created a chip on her shoulder which was hard to remove, but the benefit was in making her a most determined child with a will to succeed and there can be no doubt that this was an interesting parallel to be drawn with Charlie's early life. She has never forgotten that incident.

Her forte was athletics and her ability led to her being short-listed to run for her county, becoming the first coloured girl to do so. She wore her colour as an emblem of pride, reinforcing the desire to succeed.

When Janice was thirteen years old Sister Beaulah left the home to marry her fiancée Michael Mann who was a dental technician and Sunday School teacher and their first meeting came about as a result of their interest in the church. Janice was devastated when she heard the announcement.

Unfortunately the attitude of the children's home in such circumstances was to break all ties with the pupil and the retiring teacher. It was seen as a device to avoid comparisons with other members of staff, should any of the children form a particular affinity for one person.

Sister Beaulah had been Janice's friend and confidante who had encouraged her at school and on the field of sporting endeavour.

Sister Beaulah wanted Janice to be a bridesmaid at the wedding, but yet again bureaucracy decreed that it was simply not acceptable to select just one member from a family unit, as it would have the effect of singling out and that was not allowed.

Janice kept in touch with her friend but eventually did lose touch until much later in Janice's life. Between the ages of thirteen and sixteen-and-a-half Janice was taken under the wing of 'Pop' and 'Mrs T', otherwise known as Mr & Mrs Turner. Their own daughter was of a similar age and the two of them got on extremely well. They were treated equally, something which Janice never forgot.

In the meantime Janice achieved great things in athletics and her coach believed that she could have gone on to represent the south of England and possibly her country, but when she was 17 she had formed an association with Ralph Clayden. Janice was headstrong and like many girls of that age she felt that the association would last for ever and no-one could dissuade her.

Janice conceived her eldest child at a time when the relationship was strained, but the pending responsibility moved Janice to seek security in marriage. The children's home were extremely helpful and offered to take the child to allow Janice to continue with her studies, but haunted by the past and the inevitable thoughts of rejection, she chose to keep the child and become a full-time mother. Despite being blessed with three children the marriage was not happy, and eventually the couple parted and were finally divorced in 1978.

Janice had taken up nursing and having secured a position in Harlow in Essex at the local hospital, she had acquired her own flat. She was justifiably proud of the property although when she first moved in she had just a few clothes, ten shillings in old money and four long-playing records, but she had her independence for the first time in her life.

It was a difficult time for Janice for her three sons remained with their father, but unfortunately although she saw them very regularly she did not have the accommodation to have them at home, so to an extent she experienced a mirror image of her own childhood. She flung herself into her work and became involved in a project working with the disabled and the aged at The Leah Manning Day Centre in Harlow, where five of the happiest years of her working life were spent with great friends.

One of her colleagues was also a neighbour and her husband was involved in show-business and had become acquainted with Charlie Williams. When Charlie was in the south of England he would call and see his friend and they would have dinner together.

In January 1984 Charlie was appearing at a theatre in the locality and had been invited to stay with an old friend, Alan Coulson, and his wife Hazel. Alan was a former nightclub manager and had met Charlie through show-business. Their next-door neighbours were Pat Omara and his wife Ruth, who was one of Janice's work colleagues. They had invited Alan and Charlie around for a meal and decided to ask Janice to join them.

She had heard of the special dinner guest but she turned down the invitation at first, only to be persuaded to change her mind on the day of the dinner. It was a fateful meeting.

Janice attended the dinner party and remembers waiting with some trepidation for the star guest to arrive. Charlie appeared on time and Janice remembers his opening greeting.

"Hello cousin," said Charlie, and that one comment broke the ice.

Charlie invited his guest to watch the show and then they all returned to the house where they talked until the early hours. Janice liked Charlie, a feeling which was reciprocated for they had a great deal in common. They were both sports fanatics with a great knowledge and love of football, but most important of all, they shared a similar sense of humour. She remembers asking him how his wife put up with his continual travelling, and she admits to being rather pleased when Charlie explained that he had been separated for nearly two years.

Charlie telephoned Janice the following day and asked for her home number which she declined to give, but said that he could contact her at her work if he chose to do so. Janice did not expect him to ring, but a fortnight later Charlie was on the telephone.

There were further meetings and Janice accompanied him to his shows.   The following week Charlie invited Janice to a champagne reception and after that there was an invitation to spend the weekend with him in Yorkshire.

She had arranged to meet him at Wakefield railway station, but as Charlie was busy elsewhere he sent his old friend Gordon Beecher to collect her instead.   There were a number of such meetings when Charlie's bookings permitted, and Janice remembers an invitation to watch Barnsley play Liverpool in the F.A. Cup. Charlie was a Director of Barnsley Football Club at the time and so Janice watched the match from a prestigious place in the Directors' box.   They spent the whole match talking football, tactics and players and there was no doubt that Janice was beginning to form a considerable attachment to this most likeable of Yorkshiremen.

In 1984 Charlie was starring at the Scarborough Opera House with the great comedy show-group, The Grumbleweeds and he invited Janice to stay for the whole of her summer holiday.   In the event she contracted glandular fever which meant a six week absence from work to avoid transmission to the residents but the whole six week period was spent in Scarborough and both Charlie and Janice were hooked on each other.

On Valentines Day 1985 Charlie was working in the south of England and he had called to stay with Janice at her flat which proved an eventful meeting as Charlie asked Janice to become his partner. Janice had a good job and peace of mind and after eight years on her own, the thought of being tied down to an area far away from home gave her a great deal to think about. The other difficulty was Charlie's constant absences from home whilst working.

Janice took advice from her friends and her eldest son and she always remembers how her ex-husband was informed of the association. Ironically Ralph Clayden had always admired Charlie as a television star and comedian but apparently the only comment he could muster was "What does he see in her!"

Charlie saw a great deal in her and in September 1985, Janice finally gave up her job to travel to Yorkshire to be with him but significantly she kept her flat and rented it to a lodger, just in case!

It was a joyous union and perhaps for the first time in her life, Janice found the love and affection which she had craved.

It was not the best of starts because when she arrived in Yorkshire, Charlie was taken ill with a trapped nerve in his back and was bedridden for many weeks, but Janice's nursing abilities came in extremely useful.

The main problem was that Charlie's work took him away from home and often Janice was left at The Lodge at Birdwell on her own, so that in 1991 she decided to take a job working in a local nursing home. It was a return to nursing and the experience was entirely enjoyable, giving her something extra in her life, but it was at that time that Charlie was considering retirement. In recognition, Janice planned a surprise retirement party for Charlie, to be held at The Keresforth Hall Country Club, owned and run by their good friend John Fulton. Janice realised that she could no longer keep the venture a secret and so she mentioned it to Charlie who explained that he had not the slightest intention of retiring.

Janice was disappointed and said that she would cancel the function, but Charlie thought for a moment and suggested that they keep the booking and have a 'bit of a do'. That was Charlie's proposal of marriage!

On 28th March 1992, Charlie and Janice were married at the Methodist Church at Chapel Street in Birdwell, Barnsley, and they did indeed have their 'bit of a do' at Keresforth Hall. A large number of people turned up to the service on a day which Janice will never forget. She explained that she felt like a queen, such was the attention that they were given when it was mentioned on radio and representatives of Yorkshire Television were there to film the event. Her eldest son Terence gave her away and after the wedding they had a few days' break in Scarborough before Charlie was to start another contract.

Their married life started in considerable excitement. On their arrival at the hotel Charlie produced a bottle of champagne and promptly sent out for fish and chips for two. It was a romantic dinner with a difference.

They had planned to go out for the evening so Charlie decided to catch a nap whilst Janice enjoyed a long and leisurely bath but they were disturbed by the sound of the fire-bell. They believed it was just a drill and so Charlie continued to sleep and Janice enjoyed her bath, only to be disturbed minutes later by the hotel manager banging on their door. It was not a fire-drill but the real thing, and there *was* a fire in the hotel on their floor resulting in the next two hours being spent in the street outside the Hotel St Nicholas in their dressing-gowns!

All was well that ended well, with the hotel manager ripping up Charlie's bill and waiving any charges because of the inconvenience they had been caused. Charlie could not help but remark, "If I'd known, I would have invited all my mates in for a drink!"

So far as work was concerned, the nineties continued where the eighties left off; seven nights each week with the occasional weekend matinees included for good measure. All the balls were in the air and Charlie was able to catch each one and return it to flight, but the effort was beginning to take its toll. Tragically Charlie's health began to suffer and 1992 brought the realisation that he could no longer cope with the exacting pace which was inflicting such a deleterious effect upon his system.

Charlie the realist took over and after consultations with his doctor and a specialist, he and Janice decided that the time had come to retire from full-time entertaining.

Surprisingly enough he found the idea was easy to cope with, but the implementation proved more difficult.

Charlie's full-time career came to an end with the *'Twilight Tour'* which took the form of a number of shows at various venues beginning and ending at John Fulton's Keresforth Hall Country Club in Barnsley. The tour was a great success, and the final night was one of the most remarkable of all.

A number of celebrities turned up for the show, including members of the cast of *The Comedians* and Johnnie

Hamp. There was a telephone link which was amplified to enable the audience to hear the conversations which took place between Charlie and such friends as Cannon and Ball, Joe Longthorne and others.

When Charlie left the stage he received a tremendous standing ovation. Janice recalled, "There wasn't a dry eye in the place."

When she got to Charlie's dressing-room, she opened the door slightly to find Charlie head in hands, alone with his memories. She closed the door gently. It was some minutes before he was ready to receive guests.

Janice now organises Charlie's retirement, being kept extremely busy with their hectic social life. It is a full-time job but she still finds time to do a great deal of work for charity, particularly the local hospital who benefit from her good efforts.

Chapter Eighteen

THE 1990'S AND RETIREMENT

"It was a strange feeling," said Charlie. "After nearly thirty years of scrutinising the diary to see where I had to be the following evening, I found that I was available to travel down to Oakwell and watch Barnsley play at their home matches and, if they were playing in the Yorkshire area to the away matches too. I was able to watch the evening football matches on Sky and even watch re-runs of the old *Comedians* television programme from the seventies, which was enjoying a review on Granada Plus."

Charlie also had more time to spend with his wife Janice which may not seem of great importance to those who have never been denied the opportunity, but Charlie is now able to spend evenings enjoying the company of his wife and their friends at home or at favourite haunts in the area, without the constant pressure of a pending performance.

On three occasions in the week he plays golf at a local course where he is a member, playing the game with his circle of friends from all walks of life. He is often seen around the village where he lives, calling at the post office or simply visiting the chip shop or the local pub. Everyone knows him and everyone speaks.

He is also able to visit the cinema, something which he had missed out on in previous years, and he was rewarded by seeing his beloved county of Yorkshire move into prominence in the entertainment industry and also in films with the brilliant picture *'Brassed Off'* featuring Grimethorpe near Barnsley where Charlie once worked.   But old habits die hard and Charlie is still much sought after for concert and cabaret work and despite his retirement he is still prevailed upon to perform at charity functions and inevitably his care and concern for the locality in which he was born prompts him to make the occasional 'comeback' performance.

Charlie's aide is his old friend Neil Crossland, and together with his wife Maureen, they enjoy holidays together travelling on cruises across the world, which have been a particular delight for Charlie as they enabled him to see the sights his father spoke of so fondly in his youth.

One sentimental journey was a visit to Barbados. Charlie had always wanted to see where his father was born and had lived and he also wanted to see if there were any relatives left in the area.   In the event he visited the plantation only to be told by the manager that many of the workers were called Williams after the owners of the past so Charlie thought better of an introduction and left it at that.   It would have been nice to run into the odd relative but a village-full was another thing and he couldn't help thinking of bus-loads of people buying pints on his tab at Birdwell Workingmen's Club.   He admits that it would probably not have been such a good idea after all.

One enjoyable trip was on a cruise down the Amazon and when the ship landed at one stage of the journey, everyone attended one of the shore party trips to see the locals carrying on their everyday life in mud huts, but cynics believed that the performance had been constructed especially for the trippers. There were monkeys on the tree-lined route who were picking nuts and throwing them with remarkable accuracy at the unwelcome visitors, providing Charlie with a great deal of amusement, until they started aiming at him.

"They must have seen what colour I was. I could see them throwing at all them white people, but not at me!" The other travellers will always remember the amusing moments with Mr Williams.

So many worthy causes claimed his time, that his diary became increasingly busy and he was in danger of turning professional again. He was regularly sought out by television as a roving ambassador for Yorkshire to comment on matters pertinent to the county and its people when matters of interest required an overview.

The special concerts which he attended were always wonderful evenings and the warmth of the reception and the generosity of the applause forbade complete retirement. It was difficult for someone like Charlie who had worked hard all his life simply to stop and sit by the fireside, even though he thought at one time he might welcome the experience.

An appearance on television prompted Stanley Joseph to 'sneak' a couple of engagements into the diary for reasons which he easily explained.

"Audiences remember him and love him and it's always a great delight to book him."

Charlie cheekily, but affectionately replied,

"Aye, and he loves his percentage too!"

Charlie and Janice moved from the Rockley Lodge in Birdwell, Barnsley, because it was simply too big for their purposes but they still live in the area, in a beautiful bungalow full of warmth and welcome.   He had spent such a great deal of his time working and travelling but his spiritual home was still Barnsley where he decided to stay - most of his friends live there and *they* can understand his accent!   He keeps in regular touch with his children Melford and Beverley who live in Wakefield and London respectively.   His home is an ever open door for a huge social circle of friends of which Charlie and Janice are the centre and I am pleased to have been allowed honorary membership.

Charitable causes are never far away from Charlie's mind and with the considerable assistance of Neil Crossland he attends as many as he can to help those in need.   He feels an affinity to those whose health has been persecuted by fate and children whose future is blighted by appalling illness.

"I have been very lucky, I've had a wonderful life and whilst there have been difficult times, by and large I have enjoyed my success and have tasted the finer things in life.   It grieves me to see so many people who have not had the same luck or chance in life that I have had.   It's always been my desire to try to put something back in."

There were so many wonderful concerts and occasions when Charlie was the special guest star and I was always moved by the warmth of the reception, none more so than one evening in Brigg in Lincolnshire in the early part of 1998 when we attended a special concert in aid of a large audience of retired persons from that area.   The event was organised by some wonderful people and no expense was spared to ensure that the Christmas party was a success.

Charlie was the surprise guest and we were sneaked in by a side door so no-one would recognise him. We waited in a small ante-room to be greeted by one of the organisers, whose face lit up when he joined us and I'd almost come to expect the traditional welcome of "Ey up my flower." After a short conversation Charlie was asked if he wouldn't mind meeting the lady who had organised the catering and who was a fan, and she was party to the secret of Charlie's appearance. She was desperately keen to meet him.

Not only was Charlie agreeable to the meeting, but was genuinely delighted to see her. After a short conversation she sheepishly asked him if he would pose for a photograph with her.

"Of course my flower," said Charlie. "It would be my pleasure," and as if by magic a camera appeared from nowhere.

"Would you mind meeting my colleagues?" asked the lady in anticipation.

"Certainly," said Charlie, "I would be happy to," and a queue of some ten ladies appeared, giggling with embarrassment. Charlie was photographed with each and every one.

"Is it in colour?" asked Charlie, wearing a serious expression.

"Yes, it is Charlie," said the organiser.

"Good," said Charlie, "because if it were in black and white it would look like a negative."

During these presentations one of the organisers brought refreshments. Charlie had his customary whisky and lemonade, Neil his Coca-Cola and I had a double something or other. As Charlie was dealing with the deputations who came to see him, Neil went on stage to check the sound equipment, the curtain and the lighting. Neil is always fastidious about making sure that everything is just quite right and Charlie likes his stool centre stage and a single white spotlight. I once asked him about the lighting and he explained to me that his choice was purely personal preference. He told me that coloured lights didn't suit him, but I'm still not sure whether he was pulling my leg or not!

Neil checked the stage during a break in the concert and one of the acts was an exceptionally good ukulele player who was making his final appearance before retirement. Seeing Neil on stage and having been told who the special guest was, he remained by the curtain and as Neil fumbled with wires and the microphone he was drawn into conversation.

"It's very nice to meet you Mr Williams," said the artiste.

Neil's immediate reaction was to take the outstretched hand and shake it, but before he could answer the man spoke again.

"I've been a fan of yours for years Mr Williams," he said and then promptly picked up his uke' and left by the side entrance. Neil shook his head and completed his duties, returning to the ante-room where we were sitting. Neil recounted the story knowing that Charlie would not be offended and at the end of it, we all laughed. Then Charlie paused for a moment before observing,

"He must be colour blind."

At 9pm we were given the cue and Charlie moved onto the stage out of sight behind the curtain; the compere, called his audience to order and I was interested to hear his introduction.

"Ladies and gentlemen, now for the grand finale. You remember when the evening began I announced that we had a very special guest star to entertain you tonight. It is my pleasure and privilege to introduce to you one of the all time greats of show-business.   Ladies and gentlemen, the one and the very only Mr Charlie Williams."

Charlie walked on stage to gasps of delight from a packed audience and I was moved by the warmth of the reception.   I walked to the back of the hall, stood near to the bar and our host generously filled up my glass repeatedly with ludicrously large measures of whisky and lemonade.   It would have been churlish of me to have refused!   I leaned against a wall watching an audience of devotees, young and old, hanging on every word.   It was a lesson in observation and I suppose I spent more time watching them than him.   For a time I couldn't hear a sound;   it was as if the show had stopped for me and I was the only one who could not hear and the audience was oblivious to my presence.   I watched the faces of the people;   they were smiling.   I never thought people could smile continuously for so long with the only relaxation being the laughter as Charlie delivered the punchlines.   I could not help but notice the warmth and affection in their faces.

Charlie had been commissioned for a forty minute appearance but one hour and twenty minutes later he told his last joke and as always, left the audience with his usual expression.

Charlie took his bow to a standing ovation. The audience knew that he had only just passed his seventieth birthday and as he moved to leave the stage, a lone voice began to sing the strains of 'Happy Birthday'. She was joined by another and then another and then almost as if it had been choreographed, the entire audience joined in. It was a wonderful moment and I felt privileged to be there to see it. Charlie was greatly moved by the impromptu greeting and when it had finished he expressed his gratitude to the audience. I must confess to a lump in my throat as Charlie left the stage with the applause ringing in our ears.

I took some drinks backstage to find Charlie sitting at a table, as ever the centre of attraction. Neil asked me if I had had to pay.

"No," I said smiling.

"Bloody hell," said Neil, "I had to pay for my round, how did you get away with that?"

"Well, you're not Charlie Williams' grandson are you!" I said smiling.

Neil just nodded. He had taken the point.

The Chairman invited us to the bar, saying that a number of people had expressed the desire to meet Charlie and pay their respects. As ever, Charlie was only too pleased to agree and we walked around the side of the main hall to a door which led to the bar. The minute that Charlie appeared, our drinks were replenished and members of the audience joined us to shake his hand and to have a word. Charlie spoke to them all and was the subject of at least twenty more photographs. It meant a lot to the audience to be able to see and speak with him, and I have no doubt that the photographs which were taken that night would take pride of place in someone's album or on their fireplace or wall.

During the celebration I turned to Neil and asked him why he had not been invited to pose for photographs. I turned and winked at Charlie who smiled when Neil replied,

"It's because I was standing with you."

After approximately one hour at the bar it was time to leave. I was feeling the worse for wear and I remember turning and whispering to Charlie,

"It's been a fantastic night Charlie. I have had a wonderful time, but I'm afraid I have to admit to being pissed."

Charlie smiled and beckoned me over with a nod of his head to give me a reply which no-one would overhear.

"So am I my old son," he said, "but thankfully so is everybody else, so they'll not notice."

With a final wave Charlie left the main hall and returned to Neil's car. It had been a wonderful evening and one for the scrapbook, leaving me full of inspiration and the desire to recount the events of the day on paper.

Neil eventually dropped me off at home at about 2.30am. I went straight to my desk and started to write; waking up at 4am with heartburn and neckache. I went to bed resolving to finish the chapter by the following morning, only to find that a delicate stomach precluded me from so doing.

Brigg was one of many such concerts which I was privileged to attend and I was always struck by the incredible warmth and generous homage paid to this remarkable man, with the ability not only to make people laugh, but to genuinely like him as well. He was a man who invoked great loyalty and respect and of him it could be truly said he never had a bad word for anyone. Conversely, during my preparation of this book, I never heard a bad word about him either.

On the 27th February 1998, Charlie was top of the bill at John Fulton's Keresforth Hall Country Club, for an event in aid of the Chemotherapy Ward of Barnsley Hospital, and Janice had been heavily involved in the preparation for the show and the grand raffle. One of the prizes was a set of my books, all signed. Charlie suggested they would have been worth more unsigned, and I suppose he was right!

There were thirteen acts altogether, all vying for positions to appear in the list. One of the club acts, a male singer, was anxious to perform early as he was a milkman in his day job starting work at 5am, and so he was anxious to get his quota of sleep.

A buffet had been provided and I spent the majority of the evening talking with the other acts and picking up information and the odd story, whilst Charlie held court with some friends of the artistes who had been allowed into the refreshment area.

It was great fun to be amongst the entertainers and listen to their stories. One performer was known by his stage name of Tony Adams. He was one of the best 'vent' acts in the business and had graced the local club scene for many years. He told me of Charlie Williams, the consummate professional who was able to interest and entertain his peers as well as the audiences who had paid to see him. Charlie was a great performer and never sold his audience short. He gave one hundred per cent and people knew it. He had that special bond with an audience that only a few entertainers have and he never lost that ability.

One of the difficulties with being the star of the show is that he is invariably the last one to perform and Charlie walked up and down nervously waiting for his turn to perform.

"It's time," said the Master of Ceremonies, and Charlie walked towards the door, slightly breathless in anticipation but the entertainer who was on stage then went into a further song.

"Bloody hell," said Charlie, "I've dashed up for nowt." Charlie walked back to his seat and I walked back to keep him company. He was not concentrating too greatly on our conversation, for he had other things on his mind, but I think he was glad of the company. Then he was given his final cue and this time it was his turn. He moved nervously to the side curtains and waited for his introduction. It was an introduction which I'd heard so many times, - "the one and only, Charlie Williams."

Charlie was greeted on stage with a terrific round of applause. He went into his routine, propounding the benefits of living in Barnsley and threatening to move in and live next door to any would-be heckler.

"They asked me to appear in Roots," said Charlie, "because I was good-looking for a darky. I would have played the part of the slave who was brought from Africa, what was his name............?" Charlie gave the audience the impression that he had forgotten the central character until a lady shouted out from the back of the audience, "Kuntakinti," she said. Charlie looked across at the audience in mock disgust, implying that the lady had said something other than the name of the character.

"I beg your pardon missus," said Charlie with disdain. The audience laughed and it was some seconds before he was able to continue. His wonderful sense of timing had not left him and after a thirty minute spot, Charlie bade his farewell to an audience who had been rolling in the aisles at his banter. Before he could move away from the microphone, the audience stood as one and I witnessed yet another standing ovation. I heard someone in the audience shout, "Good for you Charlie," and I'm sure he heard it. The M.C. called him back on for a reprise before leaving with the applause ringing in his ears.

I walked into the side room to add my congratulations but before he could answer someone else had claimed his attention. Perhaps the delivery was a little slower and he didn't move about the stage as quickly as had once been the case, but intrinsically his timing had not deserted him and it was delightful to be able to watch the great comedian at work.

On 22nd April 1998, Charlie appeared before a select audience at the Rotherham Trades Club. He was guest star in a charity concert and a packed audience cheered when Charlie's name was announced. Unfortunately the gremlins were at work and the PA system was not working properly. The speakers whistled and hummed so violently that the audience winced. Eventually the sound engineer had matters under control and Charlie turned the bad start into one huge laugh. He had been making various jokes which some would consider racist and had passed some remark about the physical capabilities of certain of his brethren. The audience were highly entertained, but then the gremlins struck again and the sound of distortion reverberated through the speakers. The sound engineer had to come on stage to rectify the position and Charlie pretended that he'd not seen him. He then turned and caught sight of an extremely dark West Indian looking gentleman, with a shaven head. Charlie pretended to be shocked and shouted,

"Good evening cousin."

Winston, the sound engineer, entered into the spirit of the joke and announced,

"I've brought you a fresh microphone Mr Williams, and this should not give you any problems."

The audience warmed to Charlie's ad libs and Mr Sydney Wort observed in a whisper,

"He's got them in the palm of his hand."

Sydney writes his column in the publication, *'The Clubman's Guide'* and his knowledge of clubs and artistes is second to none. He had judged the situation correctly and he too was drawn to the apparent warmth of the audience.

He was right and just when the audience were at the peak of their enjoyment, Charlie brought his spot to a close.

Charlie was greeted with yet another standing ovation. The audience loved him and he came from the front of the stage to join Neil Crossland, only to be taken back on stage a few seconds later for a further bow.

I had witnessed a number of events such as this and on each occasion I had sensed that very special affinity that Charlie had with his audience.

When we got back to the dressing-room Charlie saw his

guests, one of whom had written a special poem and placed it in a frame. It was a simple poem but written from the heart.

Charlie accepted the gift and thanked the author most graciously. We were then supplied very generously with drinks and sandwiches by the Steward. Winston, the sound engineer joined us and Charlie thanked him for his assistance and offered him a sandwich which he declined.

"I suppose you'd like a bit of missionary lad, would you?" he asked with a grin and Winston laughed.

It was all a big joke for there was nothing racist or derogatory in anything which had been said and everyone took it in good part. Perhaps those who claim to be 'politically correct' might find the story offensive, but if Winston did not, why really should anyone else. There are those who would conclude that this era of correctness has inevitably swung too far the other way and if we lose the ability to be able to laugh at ourselves and have to spend our time watching our 'p's and q's', it will be a sad day for us all!

Having considered this remarkable life, I turn to the future and what it might hold. If I was an astrologer or owned a crystal ball that worked, I suspect I would see Charlie continuing his good works, enjoying life to the full and hopefully seeing his beloved Barnsley football team back in the Premiership.

For his part, he would simply ask for some more time to allow him to continue doing what he does best by making people laugh, and by his good works continue to provide for those less fortunate than us some measure of comfort.

I asked Neil Crossland what he thought Charlie would like for the future.

"Hair," replied Neil after a pause.

"And what do you think he deserves?" I asked.

Neil thought for a moment before replying,

"The MBE would be nice, but the OBE would be better."

There has been a great deal of lobbying of the powers that be to give Charlie an award, but so far to no avail. I would sincerely hope that the people out there who make the rules and regulations and decree what awards should be made, will take on board the arguments in support of Neil's proposition, marking the remarkable life of a thoroughly nice man who made the world laugh.

Charlie kept in the news, appearing here and there with the odd appearance on television. He was asked to appear on a programme about Caribbean immigrants for the BBC called *'The Windrush Years'* and had been booked for two days filming at the television centre. The production involved a variety show in which Charlie starred together with Gary Wilmot, who first appeared on television on the talent show New Faces. Gary has now become one of the leading lights of musical comedy theatre and Charlie regards him as being one of the brightest stars on the West End stage.

On 20 June 1998, Charlie's picture appeared in *'The Times'*. This time it was in the most bizarre of circumstances. The Danny Baker column was looking at the Brazilian footballer Ronaldo. The headline was 'Smiling Ronaldo revels in the image of a golden shot'. It was an amusing article which is reproduced in the entertaining form in which it was written and it read as follows:-

"It seems that the only cloud over a complete

enjoyment of Brazil's mastery of the planet is that nobody can quite think of who it is Ronaldo looks like when he smiles.

"The most popular choice is George Formby and I, too, went along with this consensus at first, even though I knew there was a more pertinent comparison lying deep in the national psyche.

"Now I have it. It is the visage of the former *Comedians* stalwart and latter-day host of *The Golden Shot*, Charlie Williams. Williams, of course, was in younger days also centre-half for Doncaster Rovers, but I will not be seduced by mischievous whispers about a South American washerwoman's daughter and a missing light bulb in a Barnsley social club back room.

"That said, the 'bay window' that both entertainers' upper sets of teeth form when displaying pleasure is truly a genetic long shot and, as such, bound to fuel gossip."

It features photographs of George Formby, Ronaldo and an old photograph of Charlie from his days as a professional footballer (see picture section).

Charlie doubts being related to Ronaldo, but he does remember the missing lightbulb in a Barnsley social club back room!

On 7 July 1998, Charlie was special guest at a charity concert at Skellow Workingmen's Club near Doncaster. He was presenting a cheque to a worthy cause and I was Master of Ceremonies for the night. One of my duties was to introduce him.

The show was in two parts with an interval in between. The presentation was to take place just after the interval, but it was the evening when Holland played Brazil in the semi-final of the football World Cup and understandably

as an 'ex-pro' Charlie did not want to miss it.
Consequently a portable colour television was imported
to the dressing-room for him to watch the match.   I sat
with him in-between introductions and watched his
'relative' Ronaldo go through his paces into extra time.

Just before the end of extra time, I was called onto the
stage to introduce the presentation and three other awards
to artistes who were performing on the bill, but first, I
introduced Charlie as the special guest star.   He walked
onto the stage to a fantastic reception, made the
presentations and before leaving the stage, gave an
impromptu little spot which greatly impressed the
audience.   Just as he was about to leave the stage I asked
him to remain where he was, telling him that we had
forgotten a very special award.   Charlie looked
perplexed but waited to see to whom he had to make the
presentation.

I announced the Special Lifetime Achievement Award
and the audience cheered.   He stepped forward to receive
a beautiful challenge cup which bore his name.   As
Charlie stood to take the applause someone shouted,

"Good old Charlie" and "You're the best Charlie," He
heard what they had said and within seconds the entire
audience were standing applauding.

There was no doubt in my mind that Charlie was deeply
touched by the award and the reaction of the audience.
During the applause, Charlie turned to me and said,

"I'm gob-smacked, I never expected this.   It's
wonderful!   What's the score now?"

As Charlie left the stage, the applause continued and I
called him back again to take a further bow.   As he did
so he turned to me and spoke again,

"It's down to penalties."

"What is?" I asked.

"The football match, duck egg," said Charlie taking a further bow.

And with that he walked from the stage for the last time.

When the next artiste was introduced I walked to the dressing-room and saw one of the Dutch players miss his penalty, leaving Brazil as the winners and placing them in the final once again.

With the game over I asked him how he felt about receiving such an award, and in his consummately mild manner he replied,

"It was champion. Aren't people nice?"

I couldn't help thinking that they were as far as he was concerned, but then again he did have a massive advantage over everyone else, but he had earned it.

He sat nursing his award on his way back home and we did not stay because Charlie doesn't like too many late nights; but his first job was to find pride of place in his den for the award to be on show.

It was one of those wonderful nights that stand out in the mind. I will look back in years to come and using the old cliché will be able to say, "I was there."

Epilogue

Charlie has earned his retirement and long may he enjoy it.

It is difficult to quantify his contribution to showbusiness, on the one hand it could be argued that he was a pioneer and a trend-setter, to use more up-to-date parlance, and other than that he was just lucky by being in the right place at the right time.

If the latter is true, he seems to have been incredibly fortunate three times for he has been successful in all three vocations. For my part I accept that there has been a degree of luck, but then again Winston Churchill said that 'luck is no more than good preparation'. Charlie Williams must have been one of the best prepared people around.

Another view is that he succeeded in entertainment because he was a novelty. Time and time again people have referred to his success being based on him being a black man with a Yorkshire accent. But if that proposition is true, how did he manage to stay at the top for so long without the novelty wearing off, and why is it that so many audiences hold him in such high regard?

As to the suggestion that he was only successful in the north, I would ask how did he manage to play his part in the record long-running series at the London Palladium, a venue further south than Watford? The proposition is in my opinion easily defeated.

I rather favour the premise that he was driven by such a desire to succeed that having hauled himself onto the bottom rung of the ladder, he moved upwards by a mixture of hard work, persistence, a certain amount of luck but an enormous amount of talent.

He was not one for show-business parties or late-night drinking sessions. He was never mentioned in the Sunday newspapers for visiting brothels, he didn't take drugs and rubber clothing would have irritated his skin. The material in his act did not trade in filth and he was not given to bad language. He was not extremist in his views and he was never accused of greed. He had a reputation for loyalty and straight dealing. His word was his bond.

He did take some criticism for his so-called racist jokes and over the years he did receive some letters of complaint, but they were from people who neither understood what he was trying to achieve nor the manner in which he carried it out. He highlighted the tragedy of bigotry by joking about it in such a way as to not only entertain but also to inform. By ridiculing colour prejudice and those who support it, Charlie broke down the barriers and placed himself firmly within the hearts of his audiences.

His dedication to charitable causes continues to this day and the stimulus this provides not only 'keeps his eye in' but gives him a great deal of satisfaction.

Wherever he goes he is recognised and he always has a good word for everyone. When he eats in a restaurant or just stands by the bar in a pub, people say hello. I have witnessed first-hand the backward glances and it does not require the art of lip-reading to see that they say,

"There goes Charlie Williams."

I confess that when I am with him I cannot help but bask in his reflected glory, just as Michael Joseph did all those years before in Scarborough. He has time for them all and they have a great deal of time for him. He enjoys going out and watching comedians, for he enjoys a good laugh at modern day performers such as Paul Merton and Billy Connolly.

He is still popular with the television companies and whilst we were working on this book he was the subject of Sir David Frost's *'Through the Keyhole'*. The reception he received from the audience after his introduction was nothing less than remarkable.

He will say that he is a Yorkshireman born and bred. He is proud of his county and his country and he is justifiably proud of his achievements. He would neither prostitute his views nor be drawn into taking sides on such issues of race. He accepts and propounds the basic right of one and all to be equal. He is dismissive of intolerance and even more so of extremism, for it achieves little in the equality stakes. He draws no distinction between peoples and favours no particular creed. He is without doubt one of the most balanced men there is.

It was difficult to reconcile the view that Charlie had just been lucky, but if I accept that he was lucky to get a chance at the big time, I certainly cannot accept that it was luck that kept him there. The consistent theme of all the plaudits in respect of Charlie Williams not only stems from his humour, but his ability to communicate with his audience and to be able to bring out the very best in them.

Neither do I accept that the support is only home-grown. It is true that I have seen Charlie perform in South Yorkshire when the reception has been remarkable, but the same can be said about his forays out of the county, where he has been equally as well received. I found in my research that there were few who held such a negative view, but I have examined the suggestion for fear that this tribute would appear one-sided. The difficulty I had was in finding any dissenters. I wrestled with the problem thinking that people might say I had been patronising, but I have stuck to the truth and related the facts as I found them. I was unable to detect skeletons in any cupboards and I doubt if his true fans, friends and acquaintances would have wanted me to explore the prospect.

The one question I have never been asked is "What is he really like?" It is almost as if everyone knows. The public persona is not unlike the private one, the only difference is in the presentation. When on stage, Charlie exudes warmth and understanding. Off stage he is quieter, more relaxed and contemplative. He has the air of a man who is fulfilled and satisfied with life. He has had three careers, two marriages, two children and a 'grand old time'. He has known heartache and despair, poverty and a measure of wealth. He has friends and acquaintances and a face so familiar that he is instantly recognisable, but he is neither brash nor arrogant.

Some show-business types prefer a drum-roll when they enter theatres, pubs or restaurants, but not Charlie, he prefers to keep a low profile wherever he goes. He is intuitive, quick to evaluate a set of circumstances and avoid confrontations. He will not let anyone down, his word is his bond and he would rather do a good turn than a bad one. Consequently he is popular and loved. Not bad for a Yorkshire lad who left school at fourteen.

There were sacrifices too which imposed a high price. It was met in full with interest, leaving him free to live out the rest of his life in harmony and comfort, something which I feel sure no-one could fail to wish him.

There is nothing he would really want to change even if he had the opportunity.

"I've done my best and have never knowingly hurt anyone. I've always believed that you should be good to people on the way up as you may meet them on the way down. Life is what and how you make it, rough or smooth. You have to be willing to give and take.

"I was brought up to treat all people as equal and as far as I am concerned, that is how it is. No matter what colour you are, if you are cut then you bleed with the same colour blood. Consequently I have never drawn a distinction between black, white, brown, red or yellow or any other colour for that matter.

"I have to laugh, as people spend fortunes on foreign holidays and sun lamps to get to look like me. I'm lucky, it doesn't cost me a penny. I can go to Rhyl in winter for my holidays and still come back with a tan!"

He does not really have an edge. One of his favourite sayings typifies his belief,

"It is nice to be important, but it is important to be nice."

For my part, I have enjoyed writing this book. I have been introduced to a number of artistes and characters and have made a number of new friends, to whom I am most grateful for their time and assistance.

I particularly remember Sunday 10th May 1998, when I visited the Lyceum Theatre in Sheffield on appointment to see the great Ken Dodd who very kindly had agreed to write the Foreword for Charlie's book.

He had appeared at John Fulton's Keresforth Hall Country Club in Barnsley for two nights three or four weeks previously and I attended the first show with Neil Crossland on the Friday night, and sat and watched the great man entertain a full house of devotees. I first met him in 1983, quite by chance in Vienna of all places and I reminded him of the meeting. He said he remembered it, but whether he did or not doesn't really matter. It was the thought that counted.

Charlie went to see him on the second night at Keresforth Hall and secured Ken's agreement to the writing of the Foreword. He only had to ask. I could think of no greater compliment from one of the all-time greats, such is the high regard in which Charlie is held.

But now, in true show-business fashion I have to find a suitable way of 'finishing my act'.

In all my travels and all my meetings the comment I remember best was from Sister Beaulah Mann, the lady responsible for helping Janice through her years in the home.

Her son lives in Michigan in the USA and his son, Beaulah's grandson, is five years old. He was born in England but has spent the majority of his short life in the United States. He had regular telephonic contact with his grandparents and also enjoys the visits which they make to see him.

Michael is a keen video enthusiast and she had taken a number of videos of events in England to show him. Some of the film was of their visits with Charlie and Janice which he had referred to with great pride.

Just after one visit he was asked to tell the class about his English grandparents and during the discussion he announced with great pride,

"My grandparents were born in England like me and they know a very famous Englishman called Charlie Williams."

I couldn't help thinking that, fortunately for me - so do I! It is a friendship which I refer to with great pride, having witnessed at first-hand the incredible amount of affection which is held for this man amongst his friends and his audiences.

Wherever Charlie performs, he always says farewell with his famous saying and perhaps therefore I should leave it to the man himself to finish this book in the same way.

"I cannot give you grandeur
I cannot give you wealth,
But from my heart I wish you
Happiness, contentment and good health.
Goodnight, God bless and thank you."

....and thank you too Charlie.........

TRIBUTES

I have known Charlie Williams since he was five years of age. We went to school together and worked side by side in the pit.

When he achieved great success he moved into a different circle to what he had been used to, but he never forgot his roots.

He never let success go to his head, and now in retirement he is still the same old Charlie and he is still my best mate.

Gordon Beecher
Lifelong friend and
former workmate

I remember the first time I met Charlie. It was at the time the Comedians had just started to be recorded, I think it was February 1971. I had managed to be on the first recording through being told of the details through a friend who was in the business. When I was recalled to do a second stint my agent Stanley Joseph, who was also Charlie's agent, asked if I would kindly take Charlie through to Granada as he did not know where it was, so I arranged to pick him up at a pub outside Barnsley.

I joined my pal Stewart who was driving me at the time, and we duly picked Charlie up and took him through to Manchester. I remember asking him what he would do if the TV was a success and he said,
"I am going to get a couple of years out of the TV business, make some brass and then retire."

A couple of years became a lot more!

After the first series of recordings, I went to Jersey for the season, and as the Comedians TV show wasn't transmitted in Jersey I didn't know how well received it had been, and by the time I returned in October Charlie had become such a big success. I went to see him at Batley Variety Club and you couldn't get in the place. What a great advert for the comedy business and to this day the first person people ask me about is Charlie.

My very best regards Charlie.

Duggie Brown
Comedian

When I first started taking tentative steps out of folk clubs and into cabaret, Charlie gave me some really useful advice.

Later as I got to know him a bit better I worked his club a couple of times and he was brilliant. He really looked after me, except that he warmed the audience up first and believe me, he took some following!

I like to watch the audience when Charlie is on as he has such warmth and he inspires a level of respect and affection like no-one else does, especially round here of course.

When we first saw him on The Comedians my mates and I were transfixed. There was this smart, funny, famous bloke on the telly – and he talked like us!

I have interviewed Charlie several times for radio. He has had a right life, from Upton Colliery to the London Palladium, via Doncaster Rovers. Everybody loves him, including me, and yet I have always had the feeling that I wouldn't like to upset him. I suspect that there is a rod of pure carbon steel all the way through Charlie Williams.

I'll tell you summat for nowt though; he'll do for me.

God bless Flower.

Tony Capstick
Radio Personality

I have fond memories of Charlie Williams, a great comedian and a super man to work with. We first met when I booked him to top the bill at the Opera House, Scarborough along with David Whitfield.

What a super season breaking box office records there. We toured in the autumn with my Minstrel Show and the day Charlie joined us as a guest artiste in Kirkaldy in Scotland he said, "Well Duggie, I'll save you some money this week." What do you mean Charlie?" I said. "Well, I'm the only one that doesn't have to use black make-up!" A great sense of humour, always a hit with both audiences and the artistes he worked with. I have never heard a wrong word about him from anyone who knew or worked with him, a great star with no ego at all.

When asked what he'd like to drink at a bar, he would usually ask for 'Nigerian lager', meaning Guinness! There was always a joke and it was a pleasure to be in his company.

From the shows he did for me, he still holds the box office record for 'bums on seats'. A summer at the Arcadia Theatre Skegness, a summer in Scarborough and a panto season of nine weeks in Barnsley never ever equalled Snow White.

I wish Charlie a happy retirement, but I am sure he will always be popping back for the odd date now and then. Beryl and myself wish him all future health and happiness.

Duggie Chapman
Theatrical Producer

The first time I met Charlie Williams I thought I recognised him so I asked him,
"Weren't you in Gone With the Wind?" Charlie replied, "I've got the wind, but I wasn't in the film."
I knew then that we were going to be friends!

I have to say that despite all his success, nothing about Charlie has changed, not even his act!

Nevertheless, he is still the tops. Keep them laughing Charlie, you're a lovely lad and I'd kiss you but it would only smudge my lips!

Even away from showbusiness we are still pals. Thanks Charlie for everything

Norman Collier
Comedian

It doesn't seem possible to contemplate the retirement of the 'Doncaster Bomber! It really is the end of an era in variety and clubland.

Charlie, do you remember the show we did at the Belgrade Theatre, Coventry? The Coventry Hippodrome used to have a spring and autumn variety show which was always very successful. When the Hippodrome closed, the Belgrade decided to put on a variety show to replace the one at the Hippodrome. Who, they thought, could they get to fill the Belgrade for a month in May? Williams and De Courcey came back the reply! How wrong could they be! We emptied the place. They were running away in their droves. The only good outcome was that we had to get some pints of Nigerian lager down our necks to recover our prestige. This happened every night for a month. Prestige recovered! Charlie, your retirement is a loss to the business of not only a great comedian, but also one of the few remaining gentlemen left in it. We will all miss you Charlie.

Roger de Courcey
Ventriloquist and Entertainer

harlie was really the first black stand-up comedian to crack it in this country. His achievements were simply fantastic. He opened the way for so many black performers and his achievement is even greater by reason of the era in which his breakthrough came.

On a personal level, he is such a genuine chap to whom people mean to much.

If ever anyone was entitled to star status, it is Charlie Williams.

Jimmy Cricket
Comedian

I have known Charlie Williams for nearly thirty years.

I knew him when he first started in showbusiness and following that through, his well chronicled history into the 'Big Time'.

Despite his achievements he has remained the same old Charlie, unaffected by the trappings of fame, and I suppose it was that which has endeared him to so many.

I have had the pleasure of working with many comedians over the years, but there is no-one quite like Charlie Williams.

Neil Crossland
Personal Assistant and Friend

If everyone in the world was as good as Charlie, it would be a better place to live in.

Terry Dobson
Theatre Manager

I have been very privileged to work with Charlie on many occasions and also on his last professional engagement at the Grand Theatre, Wolverhampton in October 1995.

It has always been a joy for me to watch him on stage with that charming smile, wonderful timing, terrific delivery and that lovely Yorkshire accent.

Whether playing football, golf or making people laugh he's always been the ultimate professional and a credit to showbusiness.

Good on you, me old flower!

Your friend and life-long fan,

Craig Douglas
Recording Star

Dear Charlie,

Thank you for taking part in the new series of 'Through the Keyhole'. I hope you enjoyed seeing how the film of your house turned out and that you enjoyed your studio interview as much as I and the audience did.

You were a terrific guest and I was really pleased with the final show.

I send you my very best wishes, and on behalf of the entire 'Keyhole' team, I must say what a pleasure it was to meet you.

With kindest regards.

Sir David Frost

I remember waiting in a packed queue to see Charlie Williams at a workingmen's club in the early 1970's. I also remember seeing a similar queue waiting to see him at my own establishment in the 1990's.

In the intervening years we became great friends and have spent some good times together both at home and abroad.

He has not altered one bit. He is the same old Charlie, one of the great gentlemen of showbusiness, without a bad word for anyone.

I was privileged to host the final night of his farewell tour. It was one of the most emotional evenings I have ever known.

Since then he has made the occasional special appearance and the reception he receives has never waned.

Three will never be anyone quite like Charlie Williams.

John Fulton
Night-Club Owner
And Restaurateur

O ver the years I have always taken a keen interest in the rise of 'showbiz' stars.

Charlie Williams is not what I would class as a 'showbiz' type. He has always been professional, but never lost the close contact with his public which I feel has been part of his major success.

He is of the strong character of which all great Yorkshire people are made but he remains unaffected by a success which has never gone to his head. This is why we are so proud of his accomplishments.

Christopher Good
A Charlie Williams Fan

Hy up old cock, if tha dun't behave thee sen, I'll come and live next door to thee! Britain's first black comedian talking in Barnsley twang, makes 2,000 fun-loving cabaret-goers howl with laughter at Batley Variety Club. The fact that he is sat on a toilet with a golden crown on his head is a testimony to the love and respect from the staff and cast, as well as the adoration of the public.

The resident band helpless with giggling, the bar staff straining to see what is going on unrehearsed, the rest of the cast squeezed in the wings, to watch the crowning of the King of Comedy.

Having worked in summer season with Charlie at Scarborough Opera House back in the seventies and seen him at his happiest, this is how we want to remember him – a big brusque, in your face, Yorkshireman, who having spotted a couple of young Grumbleweeds coming out of a fish and chip shop shouts, "Gerran 'addock down yer" which translated means "Why not eat a haddock!"

On complaining about the quality of an audience Charlie said "They are all good audiences." Charlie, you are wrong on that one – a lot of them are crap!

Charlie – always immaculately dressed, always warm, always funny, always with a tightly zipped wallet, always *Charlie*, tha' knows.

The Grumbleweeds
Entertainers

187

Charlie Williams is highly respected by everyone in the field of entertainment.   Not only is he a gentleman, Charlie is one of the nicest people you could wish to meet.

Yardov Hale
(alias Sydney Wort)
Clubland Critic - Clubmans Guide

As part of my work as a television producer I regularly visited theatres and clubs in search of new talent, and of course to see the artistes who were currently topping the bills. I noticed that everywhere I went, on every show I saw, there was a stand-up comedian, usually warming up the audience for the star attraction.

These comics were usually unknown to the great British public, although some were very popular with their local punters. In 1970 I had the idea of getting a bunch of these comedians into the studio to see if they could adapt their routines for a television audience.

I picked thirty comics who I had seen working at various clubs and over three nights recorded ten minutes from each of them. I took the tapes into the editing suite and made up a couple of half-hour pilot programmes using material from the best of them.

I called the subsequent series The Comedians.

A lot of the original thirty fell by the wayside, but some became stars overnight once the series was transmitted. The previously unknown comics like Bernard Manning, Ken Goodwin, Frank Carson and Charlie Williams suddenly rocketed upwards from ten pounds a night.

Charlie Williams was a hit from his very first appearance in the very first show. Apart from his excellent timing, his broad Yorkshire accent combined with his black face really caught the imagination of the viewers, as it did with me when I first saw Charlie working at a workingmen's club near Leeds.

Charlie went on to become one of the biggest stars to emerge from The Comedians. Apart from appearing in nearly every show during the first two years of the series, he appeared in the record breaking run at the London Palladium when I put together the stage version of the show.

Whenever Charlie appeared, on stage or in front of a studio audience, he extracted something extra from those watching him. They laughed at the gags of course, but there seemed to be a sort of love coming over the footlights, everything was alright with the world. Very few comedians have this power, Tommy Cooper was one.

Not long ago I staged a twentieth anniversary reunion of The Comedians and, although Charlie had not been seen on television for a long time, when he was introduced the entire audience gave him a standing ovation as hc walked on stage. The love and affection was still there after all those years.

Charlie has brought laughter to millions and has brightened all our lives. Long may he continue to do so.

Johnnie Hamp
Former Head of Entertainment
Granada Television

I wish you a long and very happy retirement. May I say it's always been a great pleasure working with you through the years. We shall miss you. You have been an inspiration to everyone. Good luck always!

Vince Hill
Entertainer

C harlie Williams is my best pal.

In the old days when we played football his career seemed to follow mine. He wasn't the most skilful player in the league but he was the fittest and had the biggest heart. He was as hard as nails and he used to say,

"You might get past me, the ball might get past me, but never both at the same time."

I can vouch for that saying!

Alick Jeffrey
Former Professional Footballer

We have acted as Charlie's agents for thirty years and although he is semi-retired we still obtain engagements for him, and of course Charlie performs at many charity functions where he is in great demand.

Of course, one must pay tribute to Johnny Hamp, whose Granada series The Comedians made Charlie an international star. His famous catch-phrase 'now then me old flower' was on everyone's lips twenty-five years ago and is still remembered today.

Although Charlie became famous through television, he was most at home playing to a live audience in cabaret and theatre. His homely Yorkshire humour and warm personality won him countless admirers.

We have not only been proud to represent a very talented Artiste, but we are proud to call him a very dear friend.

Stanley & Michael Joseph
ATS Casting

I never met anyone who didn't like Charlie. I first met him in the early seventies, just after he'd cracked it big. We were in Sunderland doing a weeks penance and we went for a long walk. I listened to his home-spun philosophies and his wise council and I realised then that there was a lot more to this bloke than what the punters saw on the stage. We used to play golf a lot then and his calming influence always raised my game from 'absolute shit' to just 'shit'. I recall once playing in a heat-wave and his head got sunburnt - it actually went red. I said, "You really are a coloured feller now Charlie."

He was never blessed with the razor-sharp wit of a Monkhouse or a Ted Ray, but he has a much bigger blessing that either of these possess and would give anything for.

From the minute Charlie walks on stage, before he even opens his mouth, you like him! His big daft grin and then that huge guffaw when he laughs at his own gags makes the audience love him.

In this age of the new wave comics using every expletive in the book and spewing forth their offensive vitriol, Charlie's innocent hilarity is still like a breath of fresh air. I'm proud to call him my pal.

Bobby Knutt
Actor and Comedian

Dear Charlie,

We all have friends.   Friends are people that we hold in special affection and regard.

Charlie, you have all the qualities we look for in a friend.   You are warm-hearted, good-natured, kind and always make us laugh — but never at the expense of others.

This is why so many people — even those who have never met you — class you as a special friend.

Selfishly, we will miss you, but you have certainly earned your retirement.

I have been privileged to meet you, but these good wishes are not just from me, but from all the many, many people in Rotherham who hold you as a friend.

**Councillor Sir John Layden, J.P. (Deceased)
Former Leader of the Council**

Hello Charlie,

It's Joe here. I had to send my very best wishes to mark, not only on your retirement, but the years of work you've devoted to the business. We go back a long way and I know I've always said it but you really are one of the true gentlemen in this profession. Keep up the golf and enjoy your retirement to the full with your family and friends. Take good care of yourself and God bless.

Joe Longthorne
Entertainer

I first saw Charlie at the world famous Batley Variety Club in the early seventies. I was in a double act at the time, just starting out in showbusiness and went along to Batley to see how the professionals did it! Charlie was the compere at the time and he absolutely blew me away! He was wonderful. I'd never seen anything like it. I'd never seen a black comedian before, especially with a broad Yorkshire accent, but it wasn't just that, he was brilliant. I could see by the reaction of the crowd that he was a star. In fact, the only way I can describe it is that he was a legend. I never forgot that night. A couple of years later I'd gone solo and was in a talent show at the Sheffield Fiesta. As luck would have it, I won! Charlie presented me with my winning plastic shield and said some words that have been burned into my soul forever. "Thas' won a talent show lad, and nas' the time to start working." I didn't quite know what he meant at the time as I was already working, but now I know - I think!

Over the years I've had the pleasure of meeting Charlie on a number of occasions and I'm always slightly in awe of him. I'm sure if I told him that he would think I was 'taking the mick' to put it politely. I've never heard anyone say anything but nice things about Charlie. Everyone loves him. To me that shows what kind of man he is. Not just a brilliant comedian. As we say around here, "I take me cap off to him!"

Charlie Williams is ranked as one of the best comedians we have ever turned out in this country and I think the Queen should give him a Knighthood!

Billy Pearce
Comedian

I first met Charlie Williams about thirty years ago. In my vocation as a journalist I spent many years writing about the entertainment scene. When I first saw Charlie he was a member of the Alick Jeffrey Duo and thereafter he became a sole singer.

I remember when he first started to add comedy into his act. On 18th May 1970 he was invited to replace a missing act at one of the heats of a competition called the Yorkshire Clublands Command Performance. Con Clusky from The Bachelors was the compere and The Nolans appeared as guest artistes. I remember that one distinguished guest in the audience was none other than the Granada television producer Johnny Hamp.

I remember it well because we were an act short only twenty-four hours before the event and we invited Charlie along, in effect to make up the numbers.

I always remember Charlie's opening words of his act when he said to the audience,
"I think you should know I'm second choice!"
Despite that he 'went down a bomb' and won the heat.

On the 10th February 1970 he appeared in the final of the competition with some of the best club acts of the day including the great comedian Duggie Brown.   Charlie was a sensation and won the title and the rest, as they say, is showbusiness history.

Apart from being a great comedian, Charlie is a thoroughly nice man.   He has time for people, consequently they have time for him.

My wife Margaret and I are honoured to be able to call him our friend.

Eric Todd
Journalist

Mayor's Parlour
Town Hall
Barnsley

Dear Charlie,

On behalf of my colleagues and myself, I would like to convey our sincere congratulations and very best wishes to you for a long and happy retirement.

During your years in showbusiness, you have done much to promote our town and I am sure I speak for the people of Barnsley when I say how proud we are of you. Your own brand of humour has certainly helped to create a good image for our town and for South Yorkshire in general.

Once again, our very best wishes to you and your wife for the future.

Councillor Judith Watts
Former Deputy Mayor

I class myself as an educated 'comedy thespian', having over three thousand hours worth of comedy tapes which I have built-up over the last twenty-five years. I love to laugh and will laugh at most things — I learned this art every morning when I got dressed!

Comedy comes in 'grades' though, ranging from adaptations on old themes to originality. Charlie is firmly entrenched in the latter.

I first saw Charlie on *The Comedians* and his style, delivery and unique sense of humour won me over as an instant fan. He was very different from virtually everybody else, and I'm not talking about his suntan either!

I saw Charlie perform live many times, but it was only in the late 1980's that I actually got to meet him for the first time. He, unlike many comedians I know, was just as funny off-stage as on it and in fact on our last meeting, at the Holiday Inn at Manchester airport where I was flying off the following morning to America and Charlie was flying off with Neil Crossland for a cruise, the wit was still abundant as he politely destroyed both Neil and I as regards my excess weight and Neil's broken leg.

Charlie is a very special man. I don't know anybody who has ever had a bad word to say about him and in this business that is nothing short of miraculous.

I never got to see him play football or display any of his other many talents apart from his comic genius, but I am personally content in the knowledge that I have come to know him as a friend, and know that he will continue to be loved by myself and millions of other people for many more years to come.

God bless you Charlie.

Rick Wakeman
Musician

I first saw Charlie Williams as a footballer. He wasn't great, but he loved the game. The second time I saw him was as a comedian on The Comedians. He was such a natural comic. The people of Great Britain adopted him straightaway. He and Ken Goodwin became not only stars of The Comedians but the biggest comedy stars in Great Britain, overnight. Comedy is about style, individuality and heart. Charlie had a bucketfull of it!

Roy Walker
Television Personality

C harlie is one of life's givers — a kind, generous and gentle man (and a gentleman as well!).

Apart from his great personal tributes he has also made a very important contribution as one of the very few British born black entertainers to pave the way for black performers in mainstream television.

My best wishes to you Charlie.

Gary Wilmot
Entertainer

Neville-Douglas Publishing Ltd
present

Plonkers
Plaintiffs
&
Pleas
by
Stephen D Smith

Plonkers Plaintiffs & Pleas is the sequel to the hilarious Boozers Ballcocks & Bail which was the first book in the comedy series relating what it is really like behind the closed doors of the legal profession. *Plonkers Plaintiffs & Pleas* continues the story with page after page of laugh out loud material.

"..Steve Smith is the legal James Herriot." - Yorkshire Post
" A hilarious book" - Charlie Williams

Pages: 256   Size: 216x135   ISBN 1-901853-10-1

Neville-Douglas Publishing Ltd
Clumber Lodge, Hemingfield Road,
Wombwell, Barnsley, Yorkshire S73 OLY
Tel: 01226 753324   Fax: 01226 758462

Neville-Douglas Publishing Ltd
present

Boozers
Ballcocks
&
Bail

by
Stephen D Smith

Boozers Ballcocks & Bail is a no-holds-barred account of the life of a thriving criminal law practice in an industrial northern town in the early eighties. It opens the door on the law in a totally honest and compelling way, giving an insight into the sometimes tragic, but often hilarious world of law courts, prison cells and solicitors' offices.

"..Steve Smith is the legal James Herriot." - Yorkshire Post

"This book will make you laugh." — Charlie Williams

Pages: 256   **Size: 216x138**   **ISBN 1-871647-33-9**

Neville-Douglas Publishing Ltd
Clumber Lodge, Hemingfield Road,
Wombwell, Barnsley, Yorkshire S73 OLY
Tel: 01226 753324 Fax: 01226 758462

Neville-Douglas Publishing Ltd
presents the book that was banned

HELL IS NOT FOR ANGELS

by
Stephen D Smith

Subject of two BBC Rough Justice Programmes

On 13 July 1990 John Megson was convicted of murder at Leeds Crown Curt. The Judge gave him the mandatory life sentence and recommended that he serve no less than 15 years! John Megson was an innocent man and it was to take five years for justice to be done.

In April 1989, a camper was fatally stabbed after upsetting members of Megson's motorcycle gang, the Druids. Megson alone was convicted of the killing and because he refused to break the bikers' code of silence he went to prison for a crime he did not commit. For two years John's fatner tried to persuade him to name the real killer. He knew his son was innocent. He then contacted Steve Smith.

A single meeting with John in Wakefield Prison convinced a solicitor with 26 years in the legal profession that an innocent man was serving a life sentence for a murder he had not committed. He realised that "I was stuck with John Megson and he with me whether we liked it or not."

Pages: 264   Size: 216x138   ISBN 1-901853-00-4

Neville-Douglas Publishing Ltd
Clumber Lodge, Hemingfield Road,
Wombwell, Barnsley, Yorkshire S73 0LY
Tel: 01226 753324 Fax: 01226 758462